Praise through the decades
for the Long-Winded Lady

"Maeve Brennan...has helped put New York back into *The New Yorker*, and has written about the city of the sixties with both honesty and affection...She is constantly alert, sharp-eyed as a sparrow for the crumbs of human event, the overheard and the glimpsed and the guessed at, that form a solitary city person's least expensive amusement."
— John Updike, *Atlantic Monthly* (1969)

"She has always been able to turn quite ordinary things into 'moments of recognition'...She does this by a steady accumulation of detail and alternate flashes of passionate statement and raw insight. The accomplishment is formidable — something few writers attempt without sounding precious, dull, or both."
— Helen Rogan, *Time* (1974)

"Reading this book I was reminded again and again of a very different one that it has something in common with — Turgenev's *A Sportsman's Notebook*. The long-winded lady and the great Russian novelist are alike in the openness with which everything — a bad-mannered dog, a little boy crying, a young man waiting for his date in the bar of what turns out to be the wrong hotel — is looked at and felt."
— William Maxwell, *Wigwag* (1988)

"Maeve had quickness of wit, a sharp tongue, and the gift of style...Bitter, dazzling, talented, tenderhearted, intractable Maeve!"
— Brendan Gill, *A New York Life* (1990)

"She was an artist of the evanescent."
— Thomas Flanagan, *Washington Post* (1998)

ABOUT THE AUTHOR

Maeve Brennan left Ireland for America in 1934, when she was seventeen. She settled in Manhattan and in 1949 joined the staff of *The New Yorker*, to which she contributed book reviews, fashion notes, essays, and short stories. Between 1954 and 1981 she wrote, for "The Talk of the Town," a series of sketches about daily life in Times Square and the Village, most of which are collected in *The Long-Winded Lady*. She gathered her short fiction in two volumes, *In and Out of Never-Never Land* (1969) and *Christmas Eve* (1974); a posthumous selection, *The Springs of Affection: Stories of Dublin*, was published in 1997. Maeve Brennan died in 1993, at the age of seventy-six.

ALSO BY
Maeve Brennan

The Springs of Affection:
Stories of Dublin

THE
LONG-WINDED
LADY

NOTE/ FROM THE NEW YORKER

Maeve Brennan

COUNTERPOINT
BERKELEY

With the exception of "The Poor Men and Women," which
appeared originally in Harper's Bazaar, all of these stories were first
published in The New Yorker. All of the stories were collected by
the author in her previous books of short fiction. Sixteen are from
In and Out of Never-Never Land, published by Charles Scribner's
Sons in 1969. "The Poor Men and Women," "An Attack of
Hunger," "Family Walls," "Christmas Eve," and "The Springs of
Affection" are from Christmas Eve, published by Scribner's in 1974.
The contents of the present volume were selected and arranged
by Christopher Carduff.

Library of Congress Cataloging-in-Publication Data is available.

ISBN 978-1-58243-501-5

Cover design by Anita van de Ven

Printed in the United States of America

COUNTERPOINT
1919 Fifth Street
Berkeley, CA 94710

www.counterpointpress.com

Distributed by Publishers Group West

10 9 8 7 6 5 4 3 2

To W. S.

CONTENTS

❋

PUBLISHER'S NOTE

✺

The first part of this book reprints Maeve Brennan's *The Long-Winded Lady*, published by William Morrow & Company in 1969. The arrangement of items, almost all of which first appeared in *The New Yorker* magazine's "Talk of the Town" department, is the author's own.

Our "Postscript" adds nine "long-winded lady" items to Maeve Brennan's original selection of forty-seven. Three of these additions — "The Last Days of New York City," "Lessons and Lessons and Then More Lessons," and "A Snowy Night on West Forty-ninth Street" — were published in *The New Yorker* as feature pieces and carried the author's byline. The remaining items were published, as letters from the long-winded lady, in "The Talk of the Town."

"A Snowy Night on West Forty-ninth Street" was included in Maeve Brennan's story collection *Christmas Eve* (1974). The other items in the "Postscript" are collected here in book form for the first time.

THE
LONG-WINDED
LADY

AUTHOR'S NOTE

✹

THE forty-seven pieces collected here were written for *The New Yorker* between 1953 and 1968. They appeared in "The Talk of the Town," where they were introduced by a phrase that varied very little from one time to the next. It was a simple phrase — "We have received another communication from our friend the long-winded lady"; "Our friend the long-winded lady has written to us as follows." Now when I read through this book I seem to be looking at snapshots. It is as though the long-winded lady were showing snapshots taken during a long, slow journey not through but in the most cumbersome, most reckless, most ambitious, most confused, most comical, the saddest and coldest and most human of cities. Sometimes I think that inside New York there is a Wooden Horse struggling desperately to get out, but more often these days I think of New York as the capsized city. Half-capsized, anyway, with the inhabitants hanging on, most of them still able to laugh as they cling to the island that is their life's predicament.

Even after more than twenty-five years the long-

winded lady cannot think of herself as a "real" New Yorker.
If she has a title, it is one held by many others, that of a
traveler in residence. As a traveler she is interested in what
she sees, but she is not very curious, not even inquisitive.
She is not a sightseer, never an explorer. Little out-of-the-
way places have to be right next door to wherever she
happens to be living for her to discover them. She has
never felt the urge that drives people to investigate the city
from top to bottom. Large areas of city living are a blank
to her. She knows next to nothing about the Lower East
Side, less about the Upper East Side, nothing at all about
the Upper West Side. She believes that small, inexpensive
restaurants are the home fires of New York City. She
seldom goes to the theater or to the movies or to art
galleries or museums. She likes parades very much. She
wishes we could have music in the streets — strolling vio-
linists, singers, barrel organs without monkeys. She thinks
the best view of the city is the one you get from the bar
that is on top of the Time-Life Building. She also likes
the view from the windows of street-level restaurants. She
hates being a shut-in diner. She wishes all the old Longchamps restaurants would come back with all their oranges and mosaic Indians and imitation greenery. She
wishes Tim Costello hadn't died. She likes taxis. She trav-
els in buses and subways only when she is trying to stop
smoking. When a famous, good old house is torn down
she thinks it is silly to memorialize it by putting a plaque
on the concrete walls of the superstructure that takes its

place. She regrets Stern Bros. department store, and Wanamaker's, and all the demolished hotels, including the Astor. When she looks about her, it is not the strange or exotic ways of people that interest her, but the ordinary ways, when something that is familiar to her shows. She is drawn to what she recognizes, or half-recognizes, and these forty-seven pieces are the record of forty-seven moments of recognition. Somebody said, "We are real only in moments of kindness." Moments of kindness, moments of recognition — if there is a difference it is a faint one. I think the long-winded lady is real when she writes, here, about some of the sights she saw in the city she loves.

1969

They Were Both about Forty

SOMEBODY said, "A full-grown child is five-sixths memory." It was half a joke, I suppose, but last night, at a quarter past nine, I saw two full-grown city children — middle-aged people — walking together on Sixth Avenue, and in each of them memory was quite suspended for the sake of the moment they were spending together. They were engrossed in each other. He was besotted. She was proud. She was far gone in hauteur, but her disdainful expression was alien to her harsh face. He was different. The state of beatitude was natural to him, and his expression would normally change only to become more or less intensely pleased with the world and with his own condition. He was from one of the Spanish-speaking countries, and I think he had been here only a very short time. She was showing him her neighborhood — Sixth Avenue in the Forties, where furnished rooms and cheap hotels are still to be found, in spite of the enormous amount of demolition that has taken place around there this year to make way for the new skyscrapers. His hair was black and dense and glossy, like boot polish, and he had big, soft brown eyes and smooth skin. He had a little half-moon mustache. He was a Latin type, and she was Hogarthian, with Plantagenet features. Her forehead was big, and she had small blue eyes, a domineering, bony nose, and a thin mouth. Her upper lip made a perfect cupid's bow — pale pink, no lipstick — but her skin had the bad, stretched look of the white cotton hand towels they give you in poor hotels. Her hair had been bleached and dyed so often that it was weathered to a rough rust-pink, and it hung stiffly down her back like a mane, or like wig hair before it has been brushed and combed and curled into shape. They were both about forty, and they were the same height (five feet four or so) and about the same weight (a hundred and sixty pounds), and they both had short legs and barrel bodies and short necks. His left arm and hand were locked in her right arm and hand. They paced along together exactly as though they were walking down the long, long aisle leading from the altar where they had been married. To look at them, you could imagine throngs of friends and relatives watching them and waiting to follow them out of the church. When I first saw them, they were approaching the northeast corner of Forty-fourth and Sixth, and were about to cross the street and continue their perambulation downtown. There were numbers of people on the sidewalk, and the full-grown children emerged from the crowd, but, more than that, they emerged from the long, dark distance beyond them. The night view up Sixth Avenue is eerie now that the

blocks on the west side of the avenue are half broken
down and half gone. It is as though the area had been
attacked and then left in pieces, and there is a clear view all
the way to Fiftieth Street, where the shimmering cliffs of
the Time-Life skyscraper stand up to be seen in their
entirety for the first time since they were built, nine years
ago. I noticed the two people because of the deliberate way
they walked, close together, and because the hem of her
dress was about three inches below her knees. She wore
a sleeveless, buttoned-down-the-front dress of pale pink
cotton printed with green foliage and cream-colored flowers, and it hung straight down from her shoulders to end
in a deep flounce. Her bare legs were heavily marked with
spots, bruises, and swollen dark-blue veins, and she wore
flat brown moccasins embroidered in white and gold, like
bedroom slippers. She carried no handbag, not even a
change purse — no luggage at all. She was close to home,
out for a few minutes, taking a little constitutional with
her friend. He attempted to match her informal attire by
going tieless and coatless. He wore navy blue trousers,
buttoned tightly around his middle, and a plain white shirt
with the sleeves folded back to his elbows, and open-toed
leather sandals that showed off his striped socks. When
the two had crossed Forty-fourth Street and were pro-
ceeding downtown, she was attracted by the model
kitchen on display in the Hotpoint showroom in the corner building, and they went to the window and stood, side
by side, looking in. It was a very fancy kitchen in chocolate
brown and ombré yellow, and the flowered partition that

served as a background wall had a "window" in it showing a summer sky and branches of dogwood in bloom. "I don't really care for that color scheme," she said, and he moved closer to her, so that their bodies were touching from their shoulders to their knees, and he turned his head and beamed into her eyes. He nodded admiringly, but he said nothing. They looked at the kitchen for a minute, and then she stepped back, and so did he, and they looked up and she read the sign over the window. "'Hotpoint Kitchen Planning,'" she read. He began to spell out the first word. *"Hotpoint,"* she said. "Ottpoyn," he seemed to say. "No," she said. *"Hotpoint."* It occurred to me that they might turn around and find me staring at them. His expression would hardly change, but hers would, and I didn't want to get in its way. When the hauteur slipped from her face, what would I see? Despair, I imagine. Not the passive, withdrawn despair that keeps itself in silence but the raging kind that incinerates all before it. I turned away and went home, leaving them to their English lesson.

SEPTEMBER 28, 1968

A Mysterious Parade of Men

THERE are more parades in this city than any of us know about. There was one yesterday that went unwitnessed and unadmired except by two policemen and me, and it was a real parade, with marching men, all in line and all in step, and martial music. This was about a quarter to eight in the morning, and it was Sunday. I was thinking about coffee, and I was standing in the middle of the block on Forty-fourth Street between Fifth and Sixth wondering whether to go along to the Algonquin, which is so small and familiar, or to walk a little farther, and east, to the Biltmore, which is so large and familiar, when I heard the music striking up on Fifth Avenue, and I hurried along to the corner to see what was happening. I can't say how many men were marching, but there were enough of them to fill the avenue for a block, leaving good margins of space all around, and that is how they were marching — neatly, keeping their margins straight. They were all dressed in dark suits, and they went shoulder to shoulder along the empty avenue, with the empty buildings and the empty windows keeping them incognito. In all these buildings, there was nobody to hear them and nobody to see them. They were passing Forty-fifth Street when I first saw them, moving along uptown at a steady tread. At that distance, they were geometric, private, and solemn, and I thought of funeral marches, drummings out of the corps, hunger marches, executions, revolutions, conscription, and strikes. One of the two policemen I had noticed was on the opposite side of the avenue at Forty-seventh Street, but the other was quite close to me at Forty-fifth. I walked along to him and asked him what the parade was. "I don't know," he said. He was very tall and pink-faced, with a cheerful smile. I said, "Have you really no idea what it is?" and he shook his head and said, "No idea." I said, "But it could be anything," and I thought of nuclear weapons, the Russians, conspirators, political plots, assassinations, and Trojan horses. The city seemed more deserted than ever, with everybody asleep, and I thought, It is just a step to chaos. I was wondering about the policeman. Then he asked, "Are you thinking of going after them?" and I said no, and turned back down the avenue and decided on the Biltmore and went over there and had coffee. The reason I had to make that choice between the Algonquin and the Biltmore is that Schrafft's is closed on Sundays.

JULY 14, 1962

The Solitude of Their Expression

YESTERDAY afternoon — I was in a taxi — I watched a very tall old man walking north on Seventh Avenue. He was passing the Metropole Café, which is almost directly across the avenue from the Latin Quarter and Playland. The Metropole is a Twist palace, and it has huge glass doors that reveal its shadowy interior. There is always something going on in there, but I have never been able to make out exactly what, because of the crowd that collects in front of the doors, people peering around

each other's heads and necks and shoulders to see what
they can see. Even in the furnace heat of yesterday the
crowd was there. It was a dreadful day. There was no air
except what was left over, and in the heat the big pictures of the Metropole's next-to-naked performers glowed
with even more than their usual fleshiness. The old man
walked past all this damp confusion as though it did not
exist. There was no contempt in his indifference. He lives
around here, and I imagine he takes Broadway for granted.
I have seen him before, but like many very old people he
looks more isolated and more fragile in this oppressive
weather. Yesterday he had left his jacket at home, and he
wore no tie. He wore a white shirt that was buttoned up at
the neck and wrists, and his trousers, which were roomy,
especially around the waist, were held up by dark striped
suspenders. His hat was made of cream-colored straw, he
wore big black boots, and his walking stick would have
marked a very firm track in the dust if that overworked
Broadway concrete ever had the chance to collect dust. He
walked in his usual way, holding himself as straight as he
could, and not going very fast. You could see his knees
working. He paid no attention to anyone and he asked for
no attention. You would think he relied on the solitude of
his expression to get him to his destination. There are a
good many very old people living in this highly charged
part of the city, which you would never think of as being
residential. The shabby side-street hotels and rooming
houses are camping grounds for all the theaters and night-

clubs and restaurants that provide the bright lights of Broadway, and some of the campers stay on awhile and then they become settlers. At present I have two big rooms in a Forty-ninth Street hotel that is sixty years old this year. I have very high ceilings and windows on three sides. My place is in the rear wing of the hotel, on the eleventh floor, and I look straight across the low roofs of the little Forty-eighth Street houses to the big flat back of another hotel that appears to be about the same age and height as this one. My hotel is twelve stories high and there is an arrangement of rooms called the penthouse on top of the roof. In the penthouse there are six bedrooms and two public baths. That hotel I see over there also has a penthouse. The hotel is made of brick, faded and dirty, pink and yellow. I don't know what the penthouse is built of, but it is painted black. It is a cabin in the sky and it makes a deck of the roof it sits on. At one end there is enough roof left over to make a terrace, which has a low stone wall that is painted a pale pink. I consider myself to be quite high up in the sky, eleven flights up, and the black cabin with its pink terrace is about on eye level with me, but as I look past the cabin, looking south across the city, the view goes up and up as the buildings go higher and higher and the walls grow more and more blank and closed. It is an irregular ascending view, split down here and there by a narrow shaft of light that shows where the big buildings do not quite meet, or are prevented from meeting by some small, stubborn survivor like the old

five-story Forty-eighth Street houses down here at my
feet. If I look over to the west I can see, where Seventh
Avenue meets Broadway, the Latin Quarter building,
which is not much bigger than a very big shed. I can see
the sidewalk by the Latin Quarter and the people passing
along, going about their business or hesitating to stare in
through the glass walls of Playland. Playland is the indoor
amusement park that takes up most of the street floor of
the Latin Quarter building. The passersby and the loiter-
ers are reflected in the glass of Playland, and there is also
reflected the constantly flowing stream of traffic on its way
downtown. That is to the west, only half a block away
from me. To the east I can see the Empire State Building
for most of its ugly length. The Empire State is at least
fifteen long blocks from here. It seems to be very close, but
then, no matter where you stand, the Empire State always
seems to have that effect of trying to be on nudging terms
with every other building in the city. The hotel with the
black penthouse and the pink terrace presents a flat, un-
adorned back full of little windows that are covered with
white curtains and shades that pull up and down. In one of
the rooms two floors down from the roof a very old lady
makes her home. I see her at her window. Now in the hot
weather she pulls her window up as far as it will go and
leaves it so, and her curtains, the white net of hotel room
curtains and worn thin, I suppose, like the ones I have
here, are fastened back so that she can get all the light and
air there is. She has two red geraniums and some sort of

very small green plant in pots on her windowsill. Sometimes she anchors a square of white cloth under the two geraniums. The cloth, stretched tightly across on two of its corners, is limp until it starts to dry, and then it comes to life with little flutters. One evening lately I saw the old lady sitting at her window, facing west or, rather, facing the west wall of her room. Her hair is completely white. She was reading what appeared to be a letter, holding it at an angle in front of her as you would a newspaper. It was one of those lucky evenings when the white summer day turns to amber before it begins to break up into the separate shades of twilight, and in the strange glow the towering outline of the city to the south turned monumental and lonely. The Empire State changed color suddenly, and lost its air of self-satisfaction. Nothing was really certain anymore, except the row of pigeons standing motionless on the western wall of the pink terrace, and beneath, the old lady calmly reading her letter. Without turning her head she put her right hand with the sheet of paper in it out the window, stretched her arm to full length, and let the paper go. It fluttered down and away, and she went on reading. There was a second sheet to the letter. She did not look out. She did not see the amber air, and she did not notice the violet blue vapor that drifted in transparency across her window, carried on a very timid little eastern breeze. A second time she stretched out her arm and let a sheet of paper go, and she continued to read. The third sheet followed the first two uncertainly down the wall of the hotel, and then she stood up and vanished at once into the dimness of her room. There was something very housewifely about the decisive way she left her window and her geraniums. She is on the tenth floor, but she might just as well have been leaving her ground-floor window after having spent an hour gossiping with her neighbors and watching the market bags to see who was having what for dinner. A good many of the ordinary ways of living go when people begin to live up in the air.

1969

On the A Train

THERE were no seats to be had on the A train last night, but I had a good grip on the pole at the end of one of the seats and I was reading the beauty column of the *Journal-American*, which the man next to me was holding up in front of him. All of a sudden I felt a tap on my arm, and I looked down and there was a man beginning to stand up from the seat where he was sitting. "Would you like to sit down?" he said. Well, I said the first thing that came into my head, I was so surprised and pleased to be offered a seat in the subway. "Oh, thank you very much," I said, "but I am getting out at the next station." He sat back and that was that, but I felt all set up and I thought what a nice man he must be and I wondered what his wife was like and I thought how lucky she was to have such a polite husband, and then all of a sudden I realized that I wasn't getting out at the next station at all but the one after that, and I felt perfectly terrible. I decided to get out at the next station anyway, but then I thought, If I get out at the next station and wait around for the next train I'll miss my bus and they only go every hour and that will be silly. So I decided to brazen it out as best I could, and when the train was slowing up at the next station I stared at the man until I caught his eye and then I said, "I just remembered this isn't my station after all." Then I thought he would think I was asking him to stand up and give me his seat, so I said, "But I still don't want to sit down, because I'm getting off at the next station." I showed him by my expression that I thought it was all rather funny, and he smiled, more or less, and nodded, and lifted his hat and put it back on his head again and looked away. He was one of those small, rather glum or sad men who always look off into the distance after they have finished what they are saying, when they speak. I felt quite proud of my strong-mindedness at not getting off the train and missing my bus simply because of the fear of a little embarrassment, but just as the train was shutting its doors I peered out and there it was, 168th Street. "Oh dear!" I said. "That was my station and now I have missed the bus!" I was fit to be tied, and I had spoken quite loudly, and I felt extremely foolish, and I looked down, and the man who had offered me his seat was partly looking at me, and I said, "Now, isn't that silly? That was my station. A Hundred and Sixty-eighth Street is where I'm supposed to get off." I couldn't help laughing, it was all so awful, and he looked away, and the train fidgeted along to the next station, and I got off as quickly as I possibly could and tore over to the downtown platform and got a local to 168th, but of course I had missed my bus by a minute, or maybe two minutes. I felt very much at a loose end wandering around 168th Street, and I finally went into a rudely appointed but friendly bar and had a martini, warm but very soothing, which cost me only fifty cents. While I was sipping it, trying to make it last to exactly the moment that would get me a good place in the bus queue without having to stand too long in the cold, I wondered what I should have done about that man in the subway. After all, if I had taken his seat I probably would have got out at 168th Street, which would have meant that I would hardly have been sitting down before I would have been getting up again, and that would have seemed odd. And rather grasping of me. And he wouldn't have got his seat back, because some other grasping person would have slipped into it ahead of him when I got up. He seemed a retiring sort of man, not pushy at all. I hesitate to think of how he must have regretted offering me his seat. Sometimes it is very hard to know the right thing to do.

FEBRUARY 15, 1958

Balzac's Favorite Food

THERE is a bookshop on Forty-eighth Street, not far from Sixth Avenue, where they sell mostly paperbacks and marked-down copies — publishers' remainders. I was in there the other day looking around. It was Saturday and the weather was cool. The shop door was open to the street. It was about lunchtime, and what business there was was casual. The afternoon was a slow one, and the city was amiable and groggy — no complaints that I could hear. Such a siesta mood is remarkable in New York City and, in the very middle of the city, strange. It was a mysterious occasion and a lighthearted one, as though all the citizens had just been given their seasonal allotment of time and had found that they had enough and to spare — plenty of time, more than they ever would have imagined. In the bookshop, all was calm. You might have been far away, in some much older city, browsing alongside the antiquarians. The pace was intent and unhurried as the customers meandered among the works of Henry James and Rex Stout and Françoise Mallet-Joris and Ivan Turgenev and Agatha Christie and the rest, more and more names turning up in front of my eyes as I stood looking. I had already collected all I intended to buy — five books under my arm — and I was looking through another book, one I cannot remember the name of, and I was reading a description of Balzac's favorite food. What he liked best was plain bread covered with sardines that he had mashed into a paste and mixed with something. What was it Balzac mixed into his sardine paste? I was just looking back to find out, reading it all again and thinking how delicious it sounded, when my ears were insulted by hard voices screeching right outside the door — people making remarks about the books in the window. "Hey, Marilyn Monroe has been reduced!" a man's voice shouted. "Five seventy-five to one ninety-two!" There were squawks of laughter, and then a woman's voice said (it was a harridan speaking), "Wait till she goes down to a dollar." "Too much! Too much! A dollar is too much!" the man shouted, and then these horrors were trooping into the shop, and I took off my glasses to get a look at them. Cruelty and Stupidity and Bad Noise — there were three of them, a man and a woman and another, but I did not see the third, who was hidden behind the tall spindle bookcase they were all looking at and making merry over. They called out names and titles, and made a lot of feeble puns, ruining the place for everybody, and I paid for the books I had under my arm, and left. I walked over to Le Steak de Paris and asked for sardines and plain bread, but when I began to mash the sardines, I couldn't remember what it was that Balzac used to mix them with. It didn't matter. Sardines with plain bread are very good. I said to myself that there was no use thinking about the hyenas in the bookshop. Their capacity for arousing violence will arouse somebody who *is* violent one of these days. (That is what I told myself.) They will trip over their own shoe-

laces. Time will tell on them. They will never know anything except the miserable appetite of envy. They will
learn, like the boy who cried wolf, that people who mock
the Last Laugh are incinerated by it when it finally
sounds. I don't care. That little bookshop stays open late,
and I am going there this evening to find that book I was
looking at that has the description in it of how Balzac
made his sardine paste. Before the evening is finished, I
will know exactly what the Master's favorite food was, and
I will also know how it tastes today.

SEPTEMBER 21, 1963

The Dark Elevator

I HAVE no great fondness for elevators at any time, and
I have developed a dislike for the two elevators in this
hotel where I live. They are perfectly ordinary self-service
elevators, safe and sound, but they carry on as though they
were dangerous. They creak, and when they stop at a floor
they bounce helplessly, and they often stop at the wrong
floor. This morning I got into one of them with even less
enthusiasm than I used to have. A few nights ago a minor
fire in the hotel left part of the top floors and both elevators soaked with water from the firemen's hoses. Since
then the elevators have smelled of smoking mattresses and
wet old plaster and cement, and the thin carpeting on

their floors is not yet dry. I live on the eighth floor, and when I got into the elevator this morning I pushed the button marked ONE for the main floor and I pushed the button marked DC so that the doors would close without delay. The doors closed quickly and the elevator began to move, and as it did so all the lights went out, the overhead lights and the signal light, all. There I was in a pitch-black box. I felt around for the metal handbar you are supposed to hang onto in case the floor gives way, but I couldn't find the bar, and the damp floor moved like grease under my feet. It was a ghastly descent. When the door opened at last, I was on the main floor and I walked across to the desk and said to the clerk, "The lights are out in the elevators." He looked at me sadly. "I know," he said. "They have been working on them all morning." He then turned to the switchboard, because in addition to being the desk clerk he is also the telephone operator, and he has other duties as well. It was very hot in the lobby. The air was old and stale, and the fan behind the desk stirred anxiously. I started for the entrance and the white marble steps that lead down to the street, but there is a public telephone booth at each side of the entrance doors and I remembered a call I should have made before I left upstairs. The phone on the right had an out-of-order sign on it — one or the other of the phones is usually out of order — and the other one held a man who was smoking a cigar. He had left the door open, and his right leg was stretched outside the booth so that he could admire his shoe, which was of straw-colored leather with airholes in it. He was saying, "Where will you be at one-thirty? I'll give you a call then. What about two o'clock, where will you be at two o'clock? Where will you be between one-thirty and two o'clock?" I sat down on a small settee to wait. The settee is covered with orange leatherette, and the wall behind it is covered with a mural-sized photograph in melancholy brown of New York City seen from the harbor. I sat sideways on the settee to avoid staring at the man in the booth, and I looked at the unreal skyline of the city I am living in, and then I stared at the end wall of the desk, which has a square hole cut in it so that the clerk can see who is entering the hotel. Decorating the hole is a potted plant about six inches high. The lobby used to be about three times bigger than it is now, but all that remains of its former grandeur is the high, ornate ceiling and the marble stairs that go off upstairs to the right. The present desk, which is very like an overturned shoebox, is cramped against the wall facing the elevators, and the end wall, between the desk and the elevators, is covered with panels of mirror that are held in place with glass buttons. One of the panels is a door that opens into a tiny office, but the door is usually closed, closing the wall. At right angles to the mirrored door, and right next to the elevators, there is a door opening into a dark and cavernous storage room, where a herd of old, worn-out television sets lie at peace and in silence. One of the television sets still has some life in it, and sometimes at night the bellman on duty leaves

the door ajar and sits on the end edge of his orange leatherette bench peering in at the performance on the screen.
At such times the night clerk on duty behind the desk puts
his elbows on the counter and watches too. I was beginning to wonder if that phone call was worth all this waiting. I didn't want to go out into the noisy, baking street
and start looking for another phone booth and I didn't
want to go back upstairs in that dark elevator. Someone
started to climb the steps from the street, and I looked
over my shoulder and saw a gray-haired lady of about
seventy who lives here. She has a room without a bath and
she is often in the hall. She has bad temper written all over
her face, bad temper and arrogance, and her eyes look
about her in a curiosity that is unkind and persistent. She
is always fighting with somebody and she is always com-
plaining. Twice I have heard her scolding the young clerk
in the grocery store next door, and I have even seen her
engage in argument with one of the tiny gypsy children
who hang around the street. She looks as though she
would like to reform somebody. It was clear, as she
climbed the stairs, that the hot weather was hurting her.
She was tired. She looked as though she had never seen a
worse day. She wore a long-sleeved knitted sweater of
beige silk and a brown tweed skirt. Her hair, as usual, was
caught tightly in a net, and she carried her handbag and a
small brown paper grocery bag. We have cooking privi-
leges here. She passed me by and stopped at the desk, but
the clerk was busy on the telephone. While she waited to

speak with him she rested one hand on the counter and
stared back at the street she had escaped from. The lobby
is not cool but it is not too bright and it is always quiet. I
think this must be the only hotel in New York City that
has no bar or shop of any kind opening off the lobby.
When the clerk had finished speaking on the telephone,
the gray-haired lady addressed him in her usual remarkable voice. She could give orders with that voice. She
asked, "Are the lights working in the elevators yet?" "Not
yet," the clerk said. "When will they be working?" she
asked. "I can't tell you," he said, "because I don't know.
They've been working on them all morning." "You told
me that before, " she said. "Is the manager in?" "I don't
know," the clerk said. "I left three messages for him to call
me," she said. "What do you mean, you don't know if he's
in?" "I know what I know," the clerk said despairingly,
"and I don't know if he's in." He then went to the far end
of the desk and hid himself in the recess there, where they
keep records. The gray-haired lady had lifted her chin
against his indifference, and she resumed her contempla-
tion of the rowdy street scene outside. She is a tall woman,
and her expression, as she realized how helpless she was,
and how afraid of the elevator, was that of an empress
confronted by the mob that has arrived to assassinate her.
She was all fortitude and dignity. Then she turned and
walked the few steps to the elevator, and as she did so her
bad temper and her arrogance and her bitterness all went
overboard and I think she took nothing into that dark and

smelly box with her except the courage she was born with.
The man in the telephone booth put another dime in and
continued with his arguing, and I got up and went out into
the blinding din of Forty-ninth Street. When I came back
later, in the middle of the afternoon, the lights were on
in the elevators and I made the ascent in comparative
security. I wonder what the gray-haired lady felt when
she reached her room. Did she feel defeat, at her circumstances, or victory, because of her behavior in the face
of her circumstances? I suppose all she felt was relief at
finding herself safe home again.

                                                    1969

Broccoli

THE luncheon hour in this city begins at eleven-
thirty; by three-thirty even those who sit down latest and stay longest have left the table. Then, until five
o'clock, the restaurants are nearly empty, and you can walk
in and arrange yourself at the table of your choice, in the
lavish solitude provided by a little sea of calm white tablecloths, and look about you, even stare, be as curious or as
indifferent or as watchful or as lazy as you are inclined to
be — in other words, be yourself in a public place and still
consider yourself polite. There is a great deal of virtue in
feeling unseen. The small restaurants I like are selfish
enough to keep the afternoon quiet hour for themselves,

so today I went to the Longchamps at Fifty-ninth Street, where there is that big window on Madison Avenue — elegant, positive Madison Avenue. I did not sit by the window. I went to a booth, halfway back in the room, that gave me a long view across the empty tables to the street. One of the booths in that Longchamps has a patched seat. It is a booth that faces the back of the restaurant. The patch, of wide gray adhesive tape, is in the form of a Red Cross cross, square and definite. It is reassuring to think of the big Longchamps chain having recourse to such a tiny, housewifely economy and being so neat about it. I sat beside that patch the last time I was in the Fifty-ninth-Street Longchamps, so it must have been summertime then, because I would never agree to face away from the window except in the hot midsummer weather, which I hate. Since that day, the year has receded by several weeks, and now it is autumn. The Longchamps menu is big and extensive, but I ordered what I always do, broiled sole with its Longchamps accompaniments, and then I looked carefully at the menu and gave an extra order, for fresh broccoli with *sauce suprême.* When the food came, the broccoli was in its own dish, with a small companion beside it — a silver sauceboat with a spoon in it. Everything was very hot. The waiter took hold of the sauce spoon and looked inquiringly at me, but I said, "No, leave it a minute." When I had finished the sole, I turned to the broccoli. I took hold of the sauce spoon, as the waiter had done, and I began to move it over the broccoli, and then I quickly put it back in the sauceboat. I could not remember which end

of the broccoli you eat. I couldn't remember. I should have
let the waiter do his job. I tried to remember other vegetables that have their limits, but their names, their appearance, everything about them, had gone out of my head. I
can think of them now — asparagus, scallions, and so on
— but I couldn't think of them then. My mind was blank,
and I could do nothing. The broccoli was fluffy, with
delicious-looking stalks. It was simply a question of where
to put the *sauce suprême*. After a while, I took the spoon
again and dribbled some of the *suprême* along the side of
the broccoli and pushed at it with my fork, and then I put
the fork down and left it so. I took up my book and began
to read absentmindedly. The waiter came and took everything away and brought coffee. He kindly said nothing
about the uneaten broccoli. There is neither moral nor
reason, and there is no justice, in this kind of private
failure, as you will understand the next time you try to
introduce two of your old friends and cannot remember
the name of one of them.

NOVEMBER 2, 1963

A Shoe Story

I WAS hurrying across Park Avenue the other day
when my left foot gave way and I almost fell, but I
recovered myself and got to the corner and up on the
sidewalk. I investigated and found there was nothing

wrong with my foot, but the heel of my left shoe had snapped in two. I was really angry, because the shoes were only a week old. A taxi was coming along, and I waved at it and got into it and gave the driver the name of the shop where I had bought the shoes. I intended to go in and confront the manager. Then I realized that I could make a much more effective stand, so to speak, if I walked in in a pair of brand-new, expensive shoes from some other shop instead of limping in in the shoes they had sold me. I asked the driver to take me to Bergdorf Goodman, and when we got there I went into the Delman Shoe Salon and told what had happened to me to the first salesman I saw, and listened to his words of sympathy. I sat down and he measured my foot, and then he went off and quickly came back with several pairs of shoes, and I decided on the pair I wanted, but I didn't like the way the bows were sewn onto them. The bows were set at an angle, and I wanted them set straight. The salesman said that the change could easily be made but that the girl who did that work was out to lunch and would not be back for twenty minutes or so. I said I would wait, and he went off with the shoes and I sat back, prepared to waste the time. I began to listen to the conversation of two ladies who were sitting near me looking at evening sandals. They were talking about the election. They were talking about Senator John Fitzgerald Kennedy.

One of them said, "He's simply too young. He's too *young.*"

The other one said, "*Much* too young."

The first one said, "Forty-three years old. It's absurd."

I began to feel very cheerful. I am forty-three. Of course, I was aware from reading the papers that Senator Kennedy and I were born the same year, but the close connection between us had never been apparent to me until that moment. I hoped the two ladies would go on criticizing the senator's age, but instead they turned their attention to the sandals and decided they didn't want any that they had seen, and they gathered themselves up and went away. That left me with nothing to listen to. There was no sign of my new shoes, so I couldn't go out of the shop. I decided I would just go up to the fifth floor and see if there was anything left from the sales that most of the stores have at this time of year. When I got to the fifth floor, I found a big sale going on. All the reduced dresses were ranged in rows on big double racks. I began to look along the rack that held my size, and I became aware that someone was humming a tune near me — someone who was hidden behind one of the dress racks. The tune was "I've Grown Accustomed to Her Face," and the humming increased in volume so gradually that it was insistent but not noticeable, the way a nice, well-treated air-conditioner sometimes is. I couldn't find a dress I wanted, and I wandered around to see who owned the voice I was listening to. It was a lady who was looking at the size tens and finding a lot of bargains. She had three dresses over her arm, and while I was looking at her she found another one worth trying on. Every time she saw something that interested her, her humming rose a little, and by the time she went off to the fitting room, with several dresses, she had almost achieved a soft chant of triumph. I have often noticed women humming when they are looking at dresses, but this lady was the most enthusiastic shopper I have ever listened to. Since I had found nothing, I went down to see about my new shoes, and they were ready, and I put them on. The salesman put my old shoes in a bag and gave them to me, and I thanked him and asked him for his name.

He said, "Mr. Sugarman," and he gave me his card.

I said, "I'd better put this card in a safe place," and I slipped it into my passport, which I have always carried since the day a taximan told me that if I was picked up for jaywalking I would be taken away in the wagon unless I had proper identification.

I said to Mr. Sugarman, "Now you're in my passport. That means you'll travel all over the world."

Mr. Sugarman said, "Oh, I hope I won't be seasick."

I said, "If you are seasick, I will let you know."

I went out onto Fifth Avenue and began to walk downtown. It was a lovely, sunny day, not too warm, and everybody was walking very fast. I passed St. Thomas Church, which I first saw twenty years ago, when I already considered myself quite grown up. I thought how astonishing it was to have been alive so many years and to have looked at so many faces and heard so many words and said so many words and seen so many different kinds of weather and still to be judged young. I blessed Senator Kennedy, and then I blessed Vice President Nixon, because he is young, too. I had friendly thoughts for everybody over forty-three and also for everybody under forty-three. I thought about the national emphasis on youth that I have often heard deplored and that I have sometimes objected to myself, and I thought that that question would not bother me again, now that I had realized that emphasis on youth really means emphasis on me. I was so taken up with myself that I walked right past the shop where I had bought my bad shoes and forgot to go in and make my complaint. Now I think I will not bother to return those shoes.

AUGUST 27, 1960

In the Grosvenor Bar

TODAY I saw the man who does the right thing in the right place at the right time and *knows* it. I think he must also be that man who is in step when all the rest of us are out of step. His sense of timing is very good. He knows when to be silent and when to speak. Perhaps he knows everything. Perhaps he has all the questions to all the answers that I have. I should have followed him. He was in the Grosvenor bar, sitting at the bar, all alone at the far end of the bar, with his back to the empty dining room that lay beyond him, when I rushed in there to get out of the rain this afternoon. I didn't exactly rush into the bar — I was washed in by a cloudburst that arrived very unfairly because it had given no warning. There had been a faint drizzle earlier, that was all. The Grosvenor Hotel stands at the corner of Tenth Street and Fifth Avenue, and I know it well because I lived around that neighborhood for years. It is a very nice bar, with small tables along the wall, and beyond it the dining room is big and has a polite hotel air. It looked very polite in there this afternoon, with all the clean tablecloths and no people. This is Sunday, and it was too late for lunch and too early for dinner. I sat down in front of one of those big windows that would look out on Tenth Street if they were not shrouded with draperies and curtains, and I was very cold, and I wondered about pneumonia. The bartender came over and put an extremely small paper napkin on the table in front of me and said, "Some rain," and I asked him for a martini. It was not too early for a martini. The man at the bar was drinking what seemed to be a Scotch-and-water. He was very middle-aged, and he had a very large face. He had his right elbow on the bar, and beside his elbow he had his black umbrella crooked to the edge of the bar. He was gazing down the length of the bar and through the glass entrance doors at the rain, and his expression was contemplative. He moved his eyes to watch the bartender mix my martini, and the bartender caught him and said cheerfully, "Some rain, all right," but he got no answer. When the bartender had delivered my drink, he went back and stood with his hand on the bar staring out at the rain and at three ladies in cotton dresses who stood huddled in the doorway. From time to time, one of the ladies would turn to look in at us all.

It was a peaceful scene until a tall, thin man in a very wet cotton suit plunged in from the street, paused to ask the bartender for a Scotch-and-soda, and then went straight back to look around the deserted dining room. He was soaked and his shoes squelched when he walked, but he was very cheerful and wore a beaming smile. He said to the bartender, "I waited twenty minutes for a taxi at the corner of Madison Avenue and Fifty-sixth Street, but I made it." The bartender shook his head and said, "This is some day for rain." The beaming man was enjoying the drink with which he was rewarding himself. He looked out into the street once or twice, and then he said to the bartender, "Is there another bar here, or any place where somebody could be waiting?" The bartender said, "Just the lobby," and he jerked his head and then pointed his arm to show the lobby entrance, which is around the corner of the far end of the bar. The beaming man squelched off and disappeared into the lobby, and in about one minute he was back, looking ruined. He said, "*This* isn't the Fifth Avenue Hotel." The bartender said, "This is the *Grosvenor* Hotel. I'm sorry, sir." And the ruined man said, "I thought it was Tenth and Fifth." The bartender said, "Ninth and Fifth, you want," and he looked sympathetic and glanced at the silent man, who remained silent. The ruined man vanished into the street. The rain continued to pour down, and the ladies outside waited patiently for it to stop. I wondered why they did not give up and come on in. No one came in and nothing happened until the silent man suddenly stood up, lifting his umbrella. The bartender said, "Thank you, sir." The silent man spoke at last, and he said, "It's a good thing it was raining when I left home; otherwise I would not have brought my umbrella." And he walked away and out, past the drooping ladies, and as he left our shelter he opened the umbrella and held it up over himself and went toward Eleventh Street, rejoicing.

AUGUST 4, 1962

A Chinese Fortune

THE train was crowded as usual last night, and so I was riding standing up with my arms clasped around the center pole of the car, and my hands were joined not together but by a copy of *Life* that I had purchased at the Fifty-ninth Street station newsstand. I was reading from the back of the magazine to the front — not from inclination, but because the particular balance I was trying to maintain between my right shoulder and the pole obliged me to turn the pages with my left hand. I describe my position with some care because it occasioned the backhanded manner in which I learned about the career of Miss Jerry Stutz and may therefore account to some extent for the unsettling effect that her remarks, which I am about to quote, had upon me. Miss Stutz is a pretty girl with dark hair who has a luxurious apartment and a French maid and a very big office. I looked at her photographs, working backward, as I say, and finally I turned to the first page of the article, where a great deal of information about Miss Stutz and her career was boiled down into one long column, and I read that she is only thirty-three years old and has recently been made president of Henri Bendel. Now, to be president of Henri Bendel is a big job for a woman of any age, or even for a man, and I was very much impressed and read right along. Here is what *Life* says, "A logical person, President Stutz likes to see perfect logic in the rapid rise to her present job. She majored in journalism at Mundelein College in her native Chicago, modeling on the side while there, and for a year after graduation wrote fashion publicity. Then she became accessories editor on *Glamour* magazine and learned all about shoes. When the $223 million General Shoe Corporation bought I. Miller shoes in 1954, it hired Jerry as fashion coordinator. A year later, breaking an industrywide tradition against woman executives, she was made vice president of Miller's and general manager of their retail stores, and sales rose 20%. General Shoe, which also controls Bonwit Teller and Tiffany, bought Bendel's and at the end of 1957 put fast-moving Jerry Stutz in

command. 'I expect it'll be years before everything's
slicked up here and I know enough to be interested in
moving along,' says she placidly. 'Meanwhile, my first
principle applies — when you come into a new job, put
your eye on people, not figures. Once you've found the
right people and set them free, you can't lose.'"

Well, I read that last sentence again, and then I read it
again. "Once you've found the right people and set them
free, you can't lose." Those words reminded me of something, but I could not remember what it was I was reminded of. "Once you've found the right people and set
them free, you can't lose." I rolled up my copy of *Life* and
fitted it into the straw carryall that always hangs on my
arm when I travel in and out of town. I repeated Miss
Stutz's words over and over, putting the emphasis on different words to see if I could discover the reason for the
commotion they were causing in my head. I am afraid my
thoughts wandered a bit. I couldn't begin to guess how
Miss Stutz recognizes a right person, but I did allow myself a little naughty conjecturing about how she sets the
right people free once she has put the finger on them.
Does she take them up on the roof at Henri Bendel? Or
out into Central Park? Does she set them free all at once,
in a flock, or one by one? At dawn, or when? If by some
mischance a wrong one starts out of a coop, how is he or
she got back in again? A hand on each shoulder? Both
hands together on top of the head? Net? What if a wrong
one gets clear away? The whole time, I kept thinking of all

the people who are right people for Henri Bendel but who
are someplace else. What arrangements was Miss Stutz
making for finding them and setting *them* free? Myself, for
instance. There I was down in the subway, but it was
entirely possible that all the time what I really was was a
right person for Henri Bendel. I was quite staggered by
the sweep and scope of the vision that Miss Stutz's words
had conjured up before me in my mundane underground
flight toward home and dinner, and I wished I could remember what it was she had reminded me of, because I
began to feel that if I didn't remember, my brain would be
locked up forever and I would never be able to think of
anything again except once you find the right people and
set them free, you can't lose.

Well, of course, it wasn't as bad as all that, but there has
been this ugly nagging in my head the last few weeks, and
from time to time I have wished that I hadn't bought that
copy of *Life* or that I had waited to get home, where I
could read it properly, first page first. Then, this morning,
I was standing at my bedroom window admiring a light
snow that fell last night and that makes everything look
much better, I must say, and suddenly I remembered what
it was that Miss Stutz had called up in my head, and
naturally it was the most trivial thing in the world — that
old, old story I first heard from a friend of mine years ago
about Chinese fortune cookies. This friend of mine told
me about a friend of hers who had dinner at this wonderful Chinese restaurant, and after dinner she ordered for-

tune cookies and the waiter brought four and she broke
them all open and read the little messages that were inside.
Well, the first three fortune cookies said, "A letter is on its
way and will arrive" and "When you are versatile, it will
give you confidence" and "Yes, you will be lucky," but the
fourth fortune cookie said, "Help. I am a prisoner in a
Chinese bakery." Well, I was really pleased with myself.
"Once you've found the right people and set them free,
you can't lose — help, I am a prisoner in a Chinese bakery." And that is all I was trying to remember all this time,
but I am so glad to have the whole matter cleared up.

MARCH 8, 1958

From the Hotel Earle

I HAVE stopped living in the country and was feeling
very pleased at the thought of returning to live in the
city, but I left the packing until it was too late to be
properly organized about it, and by the time the movers
had left to take my things to storage, where they will stay
until I find the right apartment, I was too disgusted with
my own possessions to watch the van crawl down the
driveway and too weary to be very pleased about anything
at all. Still, after the journey into town, it was very nice to
walk into the little hotel on Washington Square where I
used to stay at odd times and where I am staying now

while I look for an apartment and to notice that everything there is just the same — a familiar face, Smiddy,
running the elevator and carrying the bags and selling the
evening papers and unlocking the door and turning on the
lights and bringing the radio and admiring the waif cat,
Minnie, who could not be left at the kennel with my own
cats because she has just had kittens. It was something of a
shock to find that someone had taken a spatter gun of
white-and-gold paint to the walls and ceilings and even to
the furniture of the two rooms I used to have and that I
was accustomed to seeing in better, if battered, colors, but
the stone balustrade outside the windows, which cuts off
my view of the square but makes a good perch for pigeons,
was still hanging on, and when I looked out the bathroom
window, which does not face the square but stares straight
across at the flat side of an apartment building, I saw with
satisfaction that the tenants there still leave their shades
up at night so that it is easy to see into all the rooms, and
that the one room I like in particular, a high-up room that
has a desk against the wall just inside the window with a
green-shaded lamp on top of it, is still the same. I like that
room very much, because when all the other lights in the
building are out, the green lamp stays lighted on that desk,
sometimes with a person sitting at the desk writing, and at
night like that, with the rest of the building dead and the
square off at an angle and shadowy beyond, the lamp and
the desk high in their window make a very satisfactory city
picture.

After I had settled Minnie and showed her where her water bowl and litter box were, I washed my hands and face, reflected for a moment on the extra-sticky properties of moving-day dust, and proceeded out to dinner. I knew where I was going for dinner. I was going to the University Restaurant on West Eighth Street, but there were a couple of things I wanted to do first, and so I turned right from the hotel instead of left. I walked over to Sixth Avenue, along Sixth, and around to Eighth Street, where there is a very good flower shop, Costos, that stays open until nine in the evening. The florist said, "Long time no see," and sold me a carnation. While I was pinning the carnation on, I reflected briefly on the lack of flower shops in the country. I walked along Eighth, admiring the pastries, the lampshades, the tins of sardines and pots of jam, the leotards, the pink and red stockings, the men's clothes, the pieces of cheese, the toy furniture, and, in Politi's, the cashmeres and garnets and the handkerchiefs from France. Then I went into the Eighth Street Bookshop, where I saw not one face I knew behind the counter, but the books were there. I bought Benedict Kiely's *Poor Scholar* and a mystery story by Patricia Highsmith. I got the two books for a dollar, a big treasure and a little treasure, a dollar for the two, and as I paid for them I wondered at the curious ways of publishers, who let the good stock go out of their warehouses as what are called "remainders" almost as soon as they have it packed in. Then I was ready for dinner — books under my arm, everything in order —

but I was delayed at the curb because there was so much traffic, and while I waited an observation struggled with a hope inside my head. I was looking across at Sam Kramer's Studio, and there was the same small group of people, three or four people, hurrying up the steps, that I saw there six months ago and a year ago and six and seven and eleven and more years ago. It seemed to me that every time I have ever walked along Eighth Street I have seen this group, or one just like it, in full flight up Sam Kramer's steps, but I have never seen just one person going up. But mainly I was thinking of the small table by the window in the University Restaurant; the hope I had was that it would be free, so that I could sit there and look out at the street.

I crossed over and went into the restaurant. The table was there, nobody at it. I sat down. Bill Kravit, the waiter, said, "Been away?" and I said yes and that I wanted a martini. When he brought the martini, I ordered dinner, and then I opened my two new books, looked inside them, and began to watch the street. There are always people looking in the window of the Village Smoke Shop, across the way from my restaurant, and they were there that evening, more than usual, all looking in at something in the window. I made up my mind that when I had finished dinner I would go over and see for myself what was there. I kept looking across at the backs of the crowd and then down at one or the other of my books, and then one time I looked up and the crowd had all turned away from the

Smoke Shop to look down at the sidewalk. I could see nothing clearly except the tops of their heads, and more and more people kept crowding over to that spot where there was something more interesting than could be seen in the Smoke Shop window. A tiny foreign car was standing by the curb there, and I decided, not thinking much about it, that perhaps a dog was trapped inside the car, or that somebody had fallen asleep inside, or something like that. After several minutes, a policeman came, and his imperturbable air as *he* looked down, while everybody around looked *up* at him, told me that the cause of all the excitement, all the darting across the street to look and darting back, all the flurry and uneasiness and hesitation out there, would soon be removed, whatever it was, and I wanted it to be removed. All this time, nobody but me in the restaurant, which is long and narrow, had noticed the confusion outside, but now one of the waiters ran out and spoke to one or two people and came back in. "There's a dead woman laying across there on the floor," he said, calm and breathless. "She dropped dead." Only a few people heard him, and they paid no attention to him. "She's not dead," I said. "She just dropped *dead,*" the waiter said to me. "A woman dropped dead in the street," he said to the girl at the cash desk, who had just finished making a telephone call. A woman two tables away from me — the other tables were now empty — spoke to me. "Is there really somebody dead out there?" she said. "No," I said. "Somebody was in a car out there and they were poisoned

by gas from the engine, and now they're being revived."
The woman nodded and went back to her conversation
with her companion, and I went back to Benedict Kiely.
My coffee ice cream arrived just as the ambulance pulled
up. The ambulance doors opened, and after a short delay
some men, with the policeman hovering on solid feet,
began to lift a stretcher in. The men aimed the stretcher
badly the first time, but the second time, concentrating
with all their might, they heaved the stretcher straight into
the ambulance, and the doors closed quickly and the ambulance drove off. The policeman turned and walked away,
and most of the people in the street strolled off. I finished
my ice cream and paid my check and left the restaurant.
Across the street, I saw a woman I knew from one of the
nearby shops, and I went over and spoke to her. I asked
her if it was true there had been an accident. "A woman
had a heart attack," she said. "Quite a young woman. Only
about thirty." "But she's not dead," I said. "Oh, yes," she
said, "she had a heart attack." "But she did die?" I said.
"Yes," she said. I walked along to the hotel and went up to
my rooms. Minnie was with her kittens, but she lifted her
head when I came in and I could see her ears over the edge
of the basket and then her whole small face, her eyes
radiant with the steady, resolute anxiety of the devoted
mother. Poor waif, she had traveled a long journey with
her infants that day. She purred when I touched her, but
mechanically, it seemed. She remained on guard and I
went to bed. I hoped the woman who died on the street

had had a nice day. I don't know what I didn't hope for her.
I hoped she had no one belonging to her who loved her
enough to grieve for years, to cry all their lives over the
thought of her lying there like that. Just before I went to
sleep, I was roused by a loud screech outside, followed by
laughter — a party of people on the street, eight floors
below me. I reflected briefly on the fact that you never
hear sudden human screeches — and seldom any sudden
human sound — in the country. So ended the first evening following my return from where I was to where I am
now — home.

JUNE 18, 1960

The Farmhouse That Moved Downtown

TONIGHT, Sunday, March 6, I heard on the radio
that a two-hundred-year-old wooden farmhouse
was moved this morning from Seventy-first Street and
York Avenue all the way down to Charles Street, in the
Village — a five-mile journey. The move was a rescue.
The farmhouse was about to be demolished, because it
was in the way of a new building plan. I am staying in the
Village, and I thought I'd walk over and see the house —
see how it was standing up to its first night away from its
birth site. Charles Street is a nice street, a good place for a
house to move to. When I left my apartment, it was rain-

ing; it has been raining all day today — a long, dim, passive Sunday, with daylight ebbing from minute to minute, blurring the edges of the roofs and making the long distances of the avenues mysterious. Last night, it snowed a little, and tonight it is very dark out. I live on a small street off Washington Square Park, a street where there are always people walking, because it connects the park with Sixth Avenue, but tonight, when I walked out of my house, at a minute or so after ten o'clock, the street was deserted, wet, and lonely, and so was the park, when I glanced over there before turning toward Sixth Avenue, but the tall neon sign over Marta's Restaurant glowed cheerfully, its red color made foggy and yet intensified by the rain. Important people built these houses for their families years ago, but they have been apartments for a long time now, and Marta's is one of the old Village places that started out as speakeasies. I walked along Sixth Avenue to Greenwich Avenue, where the big open fruit-and-vegetable market is, and although it is Sunday, the market was busy, as it always is, full of color and of big, good-natured men in aprons weighing and counting and sorting oranges and apples and nuts and green peas and all the other things — pomegranates and avocados and melons, all the delicious food they have heaped up there. I stayed on Greenwich Avenue until I got to Charles Street, and when I turned into Charles I immediately began looking for the farmhouse. I couldn't imagine where they had put it. Charles is a narrow old street that starts at Greenwich

Avenue and would run into the Hudson River except that
the West Side Highway stops it. Along Charles, for the
most part, are old houses now containing apartments, and
an occasional heavy-looking big apartment building. It is
an attractive street, except that, like all small New York
streets, it takes on a dead, menacing air at night, because
of the lines and lines of cars that are parked along its
sidewalks — cars jammed together, bumper to bumper,
stealing all the life and space out of the place. Even so, it is
pleasant to walk there. Some of the residents hadn't drawn
their curtains, so I had glimpses of comfortable, peaceful interiors: corners of rooms, parts of armchairs, nice
ceilings, mantelpieces, shelves of books, paintings, people
moving about — New Yorkers at home. But I saw no sign
of the farmhouse. No sign of it between Greenwich Avenue and Seventh, or between Seventh and West Fourth, or
between West Fourth and beautiful, bountiful Bleecker
Street. After I crossed Bleecker, Charles Street seemed
darker and more deserted. I was walking toward Hudson
Street and the warehouse district — the West Village,
which is gradually becoming the best part of the Village to
live in as people slowly move away from the deteriorating
part that was once the heart of the Village. Hudson Street
is an awful street to cross, wide and grim and desolate,
like an exaggeration of a big-city highway in a gangster
movie. But when I stepped up on to the sidewalk on the
northwest corner of Hudson and Charles Street I saw the
house. It was up in the air, a ghost shape, at the end of

the block, on the northeast corner of Charles Street and Greenwich Street. The eastern wall of the farmhouse is painted a dark color, but the front wall, facing Charles Street, is white, and as I approached it I got a sidewise glimmer of it that defined the whole tiny structure. It was a *very* tiny house — much smaller than I had expected. That must have been a very small farmer who built it. It was sitting up high on a sturdy cage, or raft, of heavy wooden beams, on a wedge-shaped, weedy lot, with the old brick warehouses towering over it like burly nursemaids. It was a crooked little house — askew on its perch but crooked anyway — and it looked as plain and as insubstantial as a child's chalk drawing, but it was a real house, with real windows and a real door, and a flat roof with a chimney sticking out of it. They hadn't nailed its western wall back on — it leaned, waiting, against the nearest warehouse — but they had covered the west end of the house with a big sheet of plastic, which flapped and glistened in the rain tonight. Across Greenwich Street, the big arched windows over the loading platforms of Tower's Warehouses, Inc., stared solemnly back with a darker and more solid shine. The house was protected by a high fence of metal net, going all the way around the corner, and outside the fence, all the way around, there were yellow wooden barricades with POLICE LINE DO NOT CROSS lettered on them. The farmhouse met Importance when it arrived down here. The lot it stands on is in an angle formed by the massive side wall of an enormous Greenwich Street warehouse and the narrower side wall of an old Charles Street apartment house. Both of these sheltering walls are blank, with no windows (no eyes to watch, no sneaks to throw garbage into the lot at night), and it is as though the old farmhouse had found itself in one corner of a gigantic brick-walled garden. It is a very private place, with those big walls to the north and east, and with warehouses across both streets, Charles and Greenwich, but I saw domestic lights in the tall windows of the house diagonally across from the farmhouse, on Greenwich Street, and there are people living in the houses going back toward Hudson Street, so it is not deserted there at night or during the weekends. The house could hardly have found a better place to settle in.

It was raining very hard by this time, and as I walked away, a police car came along, driving slowly west, and the two policemen inside peered out at the farmhouse — to see if it was still there, I suppose. I walked back the way I'd come and stopped at the newsstand at the corner of Eighth Street and Sixth Avenue to buy the *News* and the *Times*. When I reached home, I read the news stories about the house, and looked at a picture showing it in its old place at Seventy-first and York, where it was surrounded by towering walls filled with apartment windows. It's much better off down here with the warehouses, and with the river so close. I read my horoscope in the *News,* and I read the gossip columns, and then I read this story:

12 STARVING CATS
SPARE PIGEON PAL

BUDAPEST, March 5 (AP) — Friendship proved
stronger than hunger for the 13 pets of an elderly
Hungarian woman. Sealed for eight days in a
Budapest apartment after their owner died, the
pets were rescued when neighbors broke in. The
neighbors found the woman's 12 cats lying around
a room, weak with hunger. The 13th pet, a pigeon,
was unharmed, although it lay defenseless in a
low chair.

Except in our minds, there is no connection between the
little American farmhouse and the Hungarian cats and the
Hungarian pigeon, but in our minds these stories remind
us that we are always waiting, and remind us of what we
are waiting for — a respite, a touch of grace, something
simple that starts us wondering. I am reminded of Oliver
Goldsmith, who said, two hundred years ago, "Innocently
to amuse the imagination in this dream of life is wisdom."

MARCH 18, 1967

A Lost Lady

I SAW a lost lady having dinner in the University Restaurant on West Eighth Street yesterday evening. She
came in alone, hurrying, with one hand up to her short,

straight silver-beige hair, which kept falling forward over her left eye. She wore a very clean raincoat of the usual light-colored cotton and a narrow dress of dark-gray linen. She was svelte and good-looking, with very white skin, and blue eyes that glanced around the restaurant with a fixed, dispassionate expression, as though it were habitual with her not to be interested. As some people give meaning to everything they touch, the lost lady seemed to look merely in order to exclude. She looked at the University Restaurant as though she were looking at a wallpaper painted to look like the University Restaurant, a wallpaper painted by a careful artist who had got everything just right — customers sitting in booths, old-fashioned costume paintings, dark and romantic, on the walls, salt and pepper shakers and lighted candles on all the tables, and, at the far end of the room, the little service bar, with the tall bartender, in his red jacket, standing ready to make drinks. Singular perspective the lady had as she looked about the room in which nothing was real except her blue eyes.

Torres was her waiter. He brought the menu and handed it to her, but she laid it down on the table in front of her without looking at it. When he asked her if she wanted a drink, she shook her head and smiled at him. "You are waiting," Torres said amiably, and he went off, perhaps not realizing that he was only a figure in the wallpaper. The lost lady smoked a cigarette. She leaned against the back of the booth, perfectly composed, obviously waiting. She was about forty-five years of age, and there was nothing girlish about her. Her husband came in and walked so quickly to her booth that it might have been the train pulling in. He was a tall, narrow man, with sharp corners for shoulders, and he smiled broadly all the way from the door. His hair was faded, shiny, and sparse, and was smoothly brushed back from his forehead. He carried one of those thin imitation-leather cases that are zippered all around and have no handle, and as he bent to kiss his wife he dropped the case on his own seat, opposite hers, and then swung himself into the booth and sat down. He must have been considered very handsome when he was about seventeen, but his clean-cut profile had been impoverished by the years, and all his early promise had atrophied in his anxious blue eyes. He looked around the room and there was no light in his eyes, although they were very eager and he kept smiling. He leaned toward his wife, nodding at her, and then he took her cigarette out of her hand, stubbed it out in the ashtray, and stood up and lifted the ashtray over onto the table of the booth behind him, which was unoccupied. Then he sat down again and reached across and caressed her cheek.

After a minute, Torres came up with the menu, and the husband took it with both his hands and began looking at it. Torres asked if he would like a drink, and he continued to read as though he hadn't heard, but then he lifted his eyes and said to his wife, "You'd like a drink, I suppose." And, without looking at Torres, he said, "A Scotch-and-water for my wife. Nothing for me." Torres went off, and I thought the lost lady's face brightened as she watched his progress toward the bar. But she didn't watch him for long. She fixed her eyes on her husband. She had come to attention when he sat down, and after he took her cigarette she had put her elbows on the table and clasped her hands under her chin. When her drink arrived, she kept one hand under her chin and lifted her glass with the other hand. She had large, even, white teeth that protruded slightly, and she kept closing her lips over her teeth and then pursing her lips, so that she looked as though she were going to give somebody a little goodbye kiss. It was a timid, flirtatious smile, and it was her only response to his chatter — because he never stopped talking. He had put his glasses on and was reading the menu carefully, mentioning certain items out loud, but as he read he also told her about the day he had had and about the people he had contended with and about what he had said to them. As soon as Torres came back, the husband looked up at him and said, smiling ironically, "Is that real onion soup or is it just something they call onion soup?" Then he looked down at the menu and up at Torres again and said, "Are the mashed potatoes fresh? Are they freshly mashed? I like mashed potatoes, but I don't want them if they've been lying around all day." He asked more questions about the food, lifting his face each time to smile and look Torres in the eye, and then he ordered his dinner slowly and emphatically, in a fussy, metallic voice of the kind that is always on the edge of a grievance. But he kept on smiling, and his wife kept smiling back at him, listening to him as he talked on and on. Only once did he pause. He buttered a piece of bread and began eating it, and as he ate he lifted the bottle of wine on the table — a bottle is put on every table at the University Restaurant — and turned it around in his hands and read the label. When the bread was eaten, he put the wine aside and began talking again — about his day and about himself and, when the food arrived, about the food he was eating. The lost lady had ordered her dinner very quickly, without looking at the menu, and she had been saying nothing, drinking her Scotch-and-water slowly until it was finished. When it was all gone, she put the glass down and looked at the plate Torres had put before her and said, "I'm not really hungry anymore." Her voice was a surprise — a clear, gentle, definite voice, with no fuzziness or drawl in it — but her tone was even more surprising, because it was the tone in which she might have said, "I am taking the shuttle to Boston" or "I am going to poison you tonight" or "It is time for a new frying pan." I thought her husband would surely stop for a minute and at least ask her why she was wasting those two nice lamb chops, but he kept on talking as though she had not said a word. It was what happens on the stage when somebody runs on and plunges a dagger into the villain, and the villain keeps right on doing whatever he has been doing, without noticing he has a dagger in his chest, because it is only a paper dagger. Her voice was all her own and made no concession whatever to her husband. I had to leave a few minutes after she spoke, and I was sorry to go, because I thought he would order Fresh Home-made Coconut Chiffon Cream Pie for dessert and I wanted to see if I had guessed right. I think one of those people was a redeemer — or a savior, if you prefer savior — but whether the lost lady married her husband in the hope of saving him from something or other or married him in the hope that he would save her from something or other I do not know.

JULY 27, 1968

The Flower Children

THIS is a Saturday in April. I am living at the moment on Washington Place, between Sixth Avenue and Washington Square Park, and this morning, when I walked out of the house, I found the street completely changed. It is a narrow little street, quite old, with enough small brownstones remaining to show what it looked like once. These days, ordinarily, it is a dirty little street — dirty and neglected and half buried under its two lines of parked cars. In fact, most of the time the street looks like a shortcut to the city dump. This morning, all that was changed. There wasn't a car in sight, and somebody had been along with a broom, and you could see the difference. Free of cars, and cleared of the debris that has been filling the gutters and overflowing onto the sidewalks, the little street looked young and light, even festive. It had taken on its first touch of festivity a few days ago, when official-looking pale green cards were tied like gardeners' labels to all the trees and lampposts. The cards were police notices announcing that there would be no parking here today, Saturday, because of a parade. This morning, a great many policemen were walking around out in the clean street, and some of them had already fenced off both sidewalks from one end of the block to the other with their low gray-blue wooden barriers. I asked one of them what the parade was about, and he said, "It's not a parade, it's a protest march." A man passing by, pushing a baby in a striped carriage, said, "It's a high school students' demonstration." It was a protest meeting against the Vietnam war, a preliminary to the huge demonstration scheduled for a week from today.

I walked toward Sixth, admiring the clean gutters. At the end of the block, one of the wooden barriers stood in the center of the street, shutting out traffic. As I reached the corner, three small boys came along, walking on Sixth Avenue past the open parking lot. The boys spotted the wooden barrier, standing alone and solid in the middle of the street, and ran over to it and began swinging on it, looking about to see if anyone would tell them to stop. Nobody bothered them, and they took a firm hold with their hands and lifted themselves up high, with their arms stiff, and then swung halfway around, so that they were

hanging there upside down, looking at Sixth Avenue and
at the traffic roaring past on its way uptown. They turned
right side up, lowered their feet to the pavement, and then
rose up and swung upside down again. They were grinning and making joyful noises at each other. Their grip on
the wood was very sure. It was a good game, but as suddenly as it had begun, it finished. The three of them
dropped to the ground and ran off, chortling, into our
local bazaar, Lamston's new five-and-ten. I went on my
way and did a few errands, and when I got back to Washington Place, there was still no sign of the protest marchers, so I went into Marta's Restaurant, in the middle of the
block, for lunch, and sat down at a table that allowed me a
view of the street. (Marta's has been going for decades, in
the basement of one of the little brownstones here, and
when the restaurant is locked up for the night — heavily
locked, behind a barricade of iron — it looks as impene-
trable as the Bank of England. But Marta's was broken
into and robbed early yesterday.) The street outside was
as it had been all morning — policemen walking about,
and a thin stream of people passing along in the usual
desultory Saturday way. I wondered where the protest
marchers were.

Then, when I was finishing lunch, I looked up and saw
that the street outside had become crowded. The protest
marchers had arrived without making a sound that I had
heard, but as I paid my check and hurried out, a voice
began to speak from a blue sound truck parked almost

directly across from Marta's. The sidewalk where I stood, just outside Marta's, was now swarming with people, all moving along very slowly in obedience to the policemen's "Move along now" and "Keep moving." The policemen looked and sounded as calm and casual as though they were keeping order in a queue going in to see a football game. There was no great press on the sidewalk, no sense of a closely packed crowd. There were people pushing baby carriages, and people carrying bundles of laundry or bags of groceries, and people walking dogs, and some who had apparently come into the block simply to see what was going on. We all shuffled along by the barriers that kept us inside, on the sidewalk, and we stared across them at the protest marchers, all of whom were very young-looking teenagers. I should think their average age was sixteen. They looked very un-grown-up. There were about four hundred of them, half of them standing in front of the sound truck and half of them behind it. The truck faced in the direction of Washington Square Park and flew the American flag. It was a very well-hidden protest meeting. Only people crossing Washington Place at one end or the other could have noticed that there was anything unusual going on. The protest marchers stood together beyond a line of barriers that had now been placed along the middle of the street, dividing it lengthwise, so that there was a clear space, half the width of the street, between the sidewalk I was on and the sound truck. The clear space belonged to the police, and they were careful to keep it clear.

The protest marchers stood close together — not packed tight, but close together — and most of them carried or wore a daffodil, and one or two carried enormous flowers made of yellow paper. They were silent. They were wearing the clothes they might have worn to school on an ordinary school day, and if it had not been for their young faces and their bright hair, they would have seemed drab. They carried no banners or placards, but a fancily lettered homemade streamer on the sound truck said HIGH SCHOOL STUDENTS MOBILIZATION. They paid almost no attention to us on the sidewalk, moving along and staring at them. For the most part, they kept their eyes on the blue sound truck.

From the sound truck a young man was calling for an end to the American involvement in Vietnam. He had dark curly hair, and he wore an open-necked shirt and a woolen pullover. He had the touch of magnetism and the sincerity and the ringing voice that make a good speaker, but he was about half a generation older than the protest marchers, and his speech sounded as though it had been written for delivery to a much older audience. When he had finished, there was a younger speaker — a young man who looked like a high school senior. He wore a tie and a jacket, and he spoke earnestly and with feeling, but he was too unaggressive to make himself heard very well. And there was a small group of girls, of high school age, who tried to get a song going. They put their heads together in a huddle and began singing very bravely, but their voices were a bit off and it was impossible to make out the words of their song. They were repeating one phrase over and over, so the sound they made was singsong and vaguely melodious, but the words were lost. The opening words may have been "A man will" or "A man must" — something like that. After singing the phrase over a few times, the girls stopped and tried to get their audience to sing along with them. One of them, a small, smiling girl, spoke up, telling the boys and girls who stood watching her that the song was very catchy, and encouraging everybody to join in. Then the little group began singing again, to dead silence, and they gave up and sang no more. Next a woman spoke who was also half a generation or more older than the schoolchildren. She was severely dressed in pale khaki, and she was vehement and appeared to be excited. She seemed to have learned her platform manner from one of those movies in which somebody tries to incite the rabble to action. Her voice sounded so hysterical that the simple occasion of listening to her became an immediate crisis that obscured any crisis or cause she might be discussing. The protest marchers watched her with no apparent sympathy.

At the east end of Washington Place, on the south corner, where the old Holley Hotel and Holley Chambers used to stand, there is now a huge New York University dormitory — a towering, well-kept building that has a luxurious aspect, at least from the outside. This dormitory is called Hayden Residence Hall. In their advertisements, real estate agents speak of ocean frontage — you have to be lucky and rich to get some of it with your house. Hayden Hall is lucky and rich in its frontage. The dormitory faces Washington Square Park, with its trees and grass and footpaths, and one side wall looks down on Washington Place, an interesting Village street even at its worst. On the sidewalk, we were all moving along so slowly, standing still every chance we got, that it took me a little while to cover the short distance from Marta's to a spot where I faced Hayden Hall, on the other side of the street. There were a few people — young men and a girl or two — up in the windows of the dormitory. They are casement windows, and very tall ones, so anybody standing up there can be seen almost full length. The university students standing in the windows could not see the sound truck or the flag unless they leaned quite far out. They stood looking straight down into Washington Place, and they seemed to be getting an enormous amount of amusement out of what they saw. The protest marchers were apparently unaware that they were being watched from above, and they continued to stand obediently where they had been told to stand. I suppose they were on their best behavior, but their best behavior seemed quite natural to them. Suddenly, from above, something hurtled down on the heads of the protest marchers, who scattered in fright — as well as they could scatter, behind their barriers. They scattered and looked at the ground and looked up. They were being pelted with large wads of white paper that had been soaked in water and now lay squashed and leaking on the street. An elderly, dignified policeman dashed over — a high officer, to judge by the brilliance of his uniform — and pointed angrily up at the windows of Hayden Hall. He wore white gloves, and his hand looked very big. Nothing more was thrown down, and after a minute or so he walked away. I left a minute or so after that. I wondered about those students in Hayden Hall. One soaked lump of paper thrown from above would have caused almost as much fright and humiliation as the two or three they threw. Why did they bother to throw more than one?

Now it is evening, and Washington Place looks its usual self again. The cars are back, parked bumper to bumper in two lines along the sidewalks, and the street has reassumed the shifty, neglected air that is typical of New York streets at night, especially in this area of narrow places. This is how the street must have looked the Friday morning, in the hour before daybreak, when a young man ran along here carrying a sawed-off shotgun. He was running away from the spot, around the corner, where he had stood when he shot away the face of another young man. The dead young man was home on leave from Vietnam. And this is how the street looked yesterday, when thieves smashed their way into Marta's Restaurant, doing a great deal of damage and running a severe risk for the sake of a few packages of cigarettes and a few bottles of liquor and a little money. I remember how the street looked this morning, when it was clean and swept and waiting, while the three little boys whirled round and round on the police barrier.

APRIL 29, 1967

Wild Money

ONE night, I found a twenty-dollar bill blowing about in the snow outside a restaurant called The Old Place, on West Tenth Street. The Old Place was owned by a lady named Theresa Tarigo, who kept restaurants in the Village for years and years and years — for decades — and this was her last place. It was down three steps, in a commodious and cozy basement, and she used to have a blazing fire going on cold nights. There was no one to be seen on Tenth Street the night I found the twenty dollars, but the night I found a dollar bill drifting along the sidewalk outside Le Steak de Paris, on West Forty-ninth Street, the block was crowded, as that block practically always is, because it leads to the theater district, and, anyway, it was a warm summer night and all the tourists in town were wandering toward Broadway and watching the Forty-ninth Street sideshow on the way. Then, last Decoration Day, I was walking along Macdougal Street toward Eighth Street. It was close to one o'clock in the afternoon, and Washington Square, the park, and

the four streets that enclose it and all the streets leading
into it were crowded with people out to see the art show
and to welcome the bright weather that had come at last
after the storm and rain of the first two days of the long
weekend. The open-air artists were grinning with joy and
turning their faces from side to side, like prizewinners, at
finding themselves in luck at last, while their paintings
glowed modestly in the cool sunlight. Outside the Hotel
Earle, beside the steps leading to the side entrance, which
has been kept locked for years, I picked up a penny and
handed it to the nearest artist — an elderly man crouched
on a campstool. He took the penny and looked at it unpleasantly, as if it were a live worm, and he was still holding it and looking at it when I wished him luck and went
on to Eighth Street — still the Village boulevard — and
so to Sixth Avenue, which was streaming with men and
women and children, who all had an air of having walked
in a festival procession from far away, from the far distance, downtown, where the roof line fades into the sky. It
was a holiday boardwalk crowd — untidy, interested, and
raffish. The artists were having an uproariously apprecia-
tive audience. I was going to lunch, taking the long
way around to Marta's Restaurant, on Washington Place.
Marta's is three steps down into a pleasant basement, as
The Old Place was, and, like Le Steak de Paris, it has a
view — a window on the street. Marta's window is partly
below street level, so what you see going by, as you sit
inside, are halves of men and women, whole children, and

dogs complete from nose to tip of tail. It is both soothing and interesting to watch people without being able to see their faces. It is like counting sheep. I never found any money outside Marta's Restaurant — no money blowing about and none lying on the ground. Somebody else got it, I suppose.

AUGUST 13, 1966

Lovers in Washington Square

WASHINGTON SQUARE PARK was being very satisfactory the other morning at six o'clock. It was a dripping green morning after a night of rain. The air was mild and fresh, and shone with a faint unsteadiness that was exactly like the unsteadiness of color inside a seashell. It was a weekday, an ordinary morning, business hours drawing near, but the evanescent appearance of the square said that anything might be about to happen — an operetta, a harlequinade, a pantomime, a fantasy about city creatures trapped by one another or about country creatures drawn to the city by dreams that turned out to be only traps they set for themselves. But, whatever the play, it would have no ending, unless to vanish is ending enough. Around the square the other morning at six o'clock there was an air of arrival and also of return. That overfed-university atmosphere was altogether absent, and

the anxiously academic façades surrounding the park
might have been made of paper, for all the reality they had.
The trees, refreshed by the night and by the damp air,
fluttered with a gaiety that seemed full of echoes — echoes of brightness, echoes of jokes, echoes of quick footsteps, echoes of friendliness. A lady who used to walk
through the park forty and thirty and twenty and ten years
ago could have walked there the other morning and found
that, after all, nothing had really changed very much.
There was a pair of young lovers quarreling helplessly —
very young lovers, a girl and a boy of about nineteen years
each. For their arena — they kept moving from bench
to bench — they had the northwest corner of the park,
where there is a large circular clearing in the grass. Far
away from them, and hidden from them by the trees, a
solitary musician of their age sat exactly in the middle of a
bench that was exactly in the middle of the long east row
of benches, so, like them, he had his back to the street,
and, like them, he looked toward grass, trees, and the
fountain. He had a bulging cloth bag, a sort of knapsack,
at his side, and he was strumming a guitar and singing to it
in a voice so low that his words were lost, though their
meaning was not. He was sad, or being sad. And behind
him, on the other side of University Place, a thin, tidy
middle-aged man had set a very small canvas on an easel
and, with his back to the sharp angle of the corner building, was intent on making his own record of the perfect
morning. By the time I saw the painter, it was a few

minutes past six. I had walked into the square from Washington Place, on the west side, and as I entered the park
I saw the girl sitting alone on a bench in her corner. Her
young man had not yet arrived. She was holding her
handbag in her lap, and she wore short black gloves. She
was dressed as though she were going to her office — in a
narrow green linen dress and high-heeled shoes. She had
an enormous mop of black hair, and her head was slightly
bent, as though she were shy and were waiting alone in a
crowded place. Then *he* appeared, strolling nonchalantly,
from Sullivan Street. He wore a brightly checked cotton
jacket, and for a man who appeared to be taking his time,
he crossed the square in very short order. As I passed by
the girl, I saw him far off, just walking into the park, and
when I turned my head he was sitting beside her — sitting
very close. But then, after a minute, she got up and walked
off across the circle and sat down on a bench that faced
him — far enough away to show him what she thought of
him but near enough for him to speak to her if he chose to
raise his voice. They sat like that, staring at each other
across the distance, the desert, for a while, and then he
stood up and walked over to her and again sat down beside
her, but this time she got up at once and went back to her
original bench and sat down, and they started staring at
each other all over again. But not for long. He got up
suddenly and walked out of the square, and she turned her
head and watched him go. He never looked back, but
when he reached the sidewalk he bent down to pat the

topknot of a tiny white poodle that was being led into the
park by its master. The poodle was so small that ordinarily
a person might stop to admire it or to smile at it, or even to
pick it up, but to bend down all the way to pat it was very
like bending down to pat a sparrow. The young man bent.
By the time his hand reached the poodle's head, he was
folded in half, and from that difficult position he twisted
his neck around so that he was looking up into the face of
the master — making complimentary remarks about the
little dog, I suppose. I imagined the girl's anguish, to see
her young man able to talk so calmly and naturally to a
stranger only a minute after leaving her sitting there alone
with a broken heart. Also, I felt her irritation with him; he
didn't seem like the kind of young man who would normally be effusive. But it was all over in a minute. The
poodle paraded joyfully into the park, and the young man
— Animal Lover, Persecutor of Women at six o'clock in
the morning — sauntered across the street and went off
down Waverly Place, heading for Sixth Avenue. He didn't
hesitate or look back, and when he was out of sight the girl
stopped watching and began waiting again. I went over to
the east side of the park, where I saw the guitarist and the
painter, and when I was starting down University Place,
leaving the Square, I looked back to where the girl had
been sitting, but there was no one there. I hope that that
girl had found sense enough to follow that young man and
catch up with him. I don't think he intended to come back.

JULY 30, 1966

I Wish for a Little Street Music

THERE are times when this city seems actually to disapprove of people. In gloomy moments, I think we are allowed to stay alive here but not to live, much less to enjoy ourselves or take pleasure in what we see when we look out of our windows or walk around our streets. If we have the fortitude to get up out of bed in the morning and get going to face the day, we should also have the freedom to rejoice, and I think the freedom to rejoice is being denied us when our senses are dulled at every turn by streets that are inimical when they are not simply sad. Tonight at seven o'clock, I stood at the corner of Forty-fourth Street and Broadway waiting for the light to change. It is a crowded place there, where a huge fenced-in parking lot occupies the site of the recently executed Astor Hotel. Broadway is dying, but the big street still looks much as it has looked for some time now — a garish architectural shambles with cheap shop fronts and a few movie houses. At seven o'clock, in summertime, the celebrated lights had not yet begun to stretch and lift and distort the scene into night's dazzling skeleton of what might have been if Broadway, the entertainment center, had been able to prove her own importance. The people crowding the sidewalks moved steadily, jostling along like sheep in a pen that has no end, except that this Broadway pen must have had an end, because some of the people were coming back. They seemed to be the same people coming back. Not that the crowd was faceless but that there was a common expression — not passive, not alert, not expectant, not disappointed: a crowd expression that conveyed nothing because it said nothing. There were few, if any, tourists in the crowd, and it was not a holiday night, not even a weekend night. The people on the sidewalks were ordinary New Yorkers after working hours. I thought to myself: All these people are sheep and I am a sheep. Somebody behind me gave a push, but I did not look around, for fear they might become angry and push me again. Instead, I watched the light and I thought: There are too many people in this world. I looked up. Over there the pale moon was rising to meet the night. At that moment I wished very much for a little street music: a man with a melodeon, or a brass band, or a piper, or a barrel organ, or a person with a big voice and a tuneful song — something surprising and friendly. The light changed and I started across Broadway along with the rest of the people who had been waiting. I was about halfway across when I heard a wild shout of "Father, Father!" and a young man ran forward so that I only saw his back. He was a very tall young man, fat and untidy in a tweed jacket that was too short for him, and gray flannel trousers, and he ran as awkwardly as though he had seven arms and seven legs to control instead of only two of each. He seemed to be keeping all his knees high in the air, and he held one arm up, like Mercury. Then I saw, on the corner, a middle-aged man standing alone with his hands clasped patiently in front of him. The middle-aged man was not very tall, and he was very thin and trim and distinct in a dark blue suit, a white shirt, and a dark tie. His face was pale, and his expression was solemn and almost stern. When he caught sight of his son, he pursed his lips into an odd smile that was half formal and half shy, and he extended his hand very formally in greeting. But then, as the son ran up and took his hand, the father couldn't help himself and he began grinning. The son bent and kissed his father, who kissed him back, and as they moved from the corner I saw that the son wasn't a young man at all but a young boy, not more than fifteen years old, maybe sixteen, and that he wasn't fat but simply growing in all directions at once. His hair was rumpled, and as he talked, gesticulating with his arms and chattering at full speed, he kept putting one big hand flat on the top of his head and holding it there, hoping not to grow another inch just yet, I suppose. He wore big spectacles, and his face was red and shiny. He had his father's brown eyes and his father's straight, narrow nose and perhaps his father's serious mouth, but it was hard to tell about that, because he was smiling and talking so much. They moved along slowly, going north, when suddenly the son remembered something more he wanted to say, and he scrambled around in front of his father and started all over again, talking and waving his arms and getting in the way just as he must have often done not long ago, when he was a small boy. The father stared admiringly up at his son, hearing every word, and you could see that what he longed for was to have the chance, just once again, to pick his child up and walk a few steps with him in his arms. And it would have taken very little to cause that boy to embrace his father and whirl him around in the air. What a funny trick Time had played on those two — or was it a trick of Light that made the son so big while the father remained the size he had been? It was as though some cameraman had enlarged a picture of the child and left the father life-size. They got themselves side by side again and went on up the avenue and were lost to my view in the crowd that was gathered outside the Criterion Theatre. I think they were going to have dinner someplace. Maybe they went to the Howard Johnson's at Forty-sixth Street. That is a nice place, especially if you get near the window, so that you can look out at the crowd passing and see that at a little distance there are no sheep on Broadway.

JULY 13, 1968

Jobs

I HAVE temporary residence in one of those small old houses on Tenth Street, just off Fifth Avenue, and this morning, when I walked out into the smothering summer weather, I saw that the showers that fell last night had made a difference after all. Last night, it seemed that

the rain had come only to disappoint us, there was so little
of it, but this morning I saw that enough water had fallen
to leave traces in the gutter, where the pigeons and sparrows hopped around, getting their beaks wet and, in one
case, at least, managing an enthusiastic bath. Yesterday, in
the same place, beside a spindly city tree, I saw a sparrow.
Parched and weightless, he fluttered along ahead of me
like a ball of gray dust, and this morning I thought that in
spite of the heat the happiness of the birds provided a
definite start for the day. There in the hospitable gutter the
birds knew themselves again. I left them and continued
toward Sixth Avenue, finding the way familiar, although it
has been years since I lived here, and the big, shabby
studio building that used to stand on the north side of the
block has been thrown down and carted away to make
room for a particularly showy apartment house. The lower
wall of the apartment house is plastered with tiny tiles,
about the size of postage stamps, in various shades of
green, and here and there small patches of raw cement
show how the tiles drop off. They drop off in ones and
twos. There is a drugstore on the corner of Tenth and
Sixth, and I went in there to get a package of cigarettes. It
is a nice, friendly place, a neighborhood drugstore. The
soda fountain is on the right as you go in, and the drug
counter, where you buy everything, is on the left. Both
counters run the length of the store, and the whole middle
of the floor, all the way down the store, is given over to
showcases and to those revolving racks where they keep

paperback books. When you sit at the soda fountain, you face a mirror that has signs on it advertising sandwiches, hot plates, and ice cream, and when you stand at the drug counter you face a wall of crowded shelves that are packed with bottles and jars and packages and boxes, but you never see the full expanse of the shelves, because the counter is lined with display cases and boxes, with a little space left free so that the clerk can see out to speak to customers and wait on them. The air was cool in the store that morning, and the bright electric lights seemed mild after the hot glare of the sunshine outside. In weather like this, when the temperature is up to nearly a hundred, and when you are in a cool place, you look at the people as they come in from the outside exactly as you would look at fellow survivors of some disaster. A boy came in from the street, and he came in so briskly and walked with such spirit that you would have looked at him no matter where you were. He was about sixteen. He wore only a shirt and trousers, but his shirt was very white and his trousers were neatly belted, and he held himself very straight. He was a tidy, happy boy. While he waited by the counter, he glanced about the store, a glance of curiosity, but he looked impersonal and triumphant, the way children sometimes look when they see something that they like but do not want. He took a flat leather wallet out of his hip pocket and began slapping it against his left hand, and when the clerk appeared he took a crisply folded paper out of the wallet and handed it across the counter. The clerk read the paper and then he handed it back to the boy. It was a half sheet of business stationery with the name of the firm, or whatever it was, in heavy black lettering across the top. "That's no good," the clerk said. "I can't accept that signature. It has to be signed here." "But it is signed," the boy said. "It has to be signed here, in front of me," the clerk said. The boy tried to hand the paper across the counter again, but the clerk shook his head. "I tell you it's no good," he said. "I thought if you saw the letterhead," the boy said. "Look, I can't help you," the clerk said, and he leaned out to speak to a woman who was waiting behind the boy, but the boy interrupted him. "What if I sign it?" he asked. The clerk looked at him helplessly. "How often do I have to tell you?" he said. "I can't help you. Look, I've got a customer waiting." The boy moved away and began to study the paper as though it had turned out to be written in a language he did not understand. When he left the store, he was still holding the paper, unfolded, in his hand. Sixth Avenue, which is loud and ugly for every inch of the long path it cuts through the city, must have seemed hideous to him, if only because he found himself there at a wrong moment in his life. He kept looking down at the paper and then looking up and down the avenue. He did not know where to turn. He was only a boy, and his imagination was shaking along with his trust in himself. He was ashamed. I could see him through the glass door, and I was also able to see the heat showing itself in the heaviness of the air and in the exhausted faces of the people walking by. A woman walked by looking as though she might faint if she took her eyes off the distance, and when she had gone, the boy, who had been standing with his back to the drugstore, walked over to the curb and turned and looked above the drugstore windows to where the name is, and I saw his gaze go on up to the red brick walls beyond. Then he folded his paper and went off, walking uptown.

Three weeks ago, on a Saturday morning, about nine-thirty, I saw someone else trying to get his bearings from a piece of paper. This was a man on West Forty-eighth Street between Sixth and Seventh, but nearer to Seventh. There is a nest of small houses flourishing there in the shadow of the big Broadway lights. The man was standing on the south side of the street, beside a handsome green delivery van that had ICE, DRY ICE, ICE CUBES in very large letters on its side. It was the only car on the block, which is usually choked with vans and trucks trying to make deliveries and with traffic moving eastward across the island. No New York street is busier or noisier or, in this block, more garish, than Forty-eighth Street. But this was a Saturday morning in summer and things were quiet. The restaurants that take up the ground floors of most of those little houses would open for lunch, but it was nowhere near lunchtime yet. When I first saw the man, he had his back to the delivery van and he was studying first a piece of paper in his hand and then the numbers on the house doors nearest to him and over the restaurants. He looked from the building where Zucca's Restaurant used to be, the one with the blue door and the small balcony above it, to a restaurant called Puerto Sagua, and so on along, but he did not move from the van. Then he turned and began to study the fronts of the houses across the street from him. He was young and black, twenty-four or twenty-five years old, and he wore no hat, and he had on a navy blue suit that was a little bit too big for him. He looked anxiously at the houses across the street from him, and he even looked at a parking lot next to the houses, as if he wondered whether the number he was looking for belonged to a house that had vanished from there. They must have torn down two or three houses to make that gap in the street where the parking lot is. It was because of the gap that I was able to see him. I was living on the eleventh floor at the back of a sixty-year-old house that faces Forty-ninth Street. At the back — that is where the view is. I could look straight down onto the flat, worn roofs of the low buildings the man was searching with his eyes, and by looking to the right, across a parking lot, I could see Forty-eighth Street — both sides of the street. There was only one car in the parking lot that morning, and it was huddled away in a corner, as though somebody had forgotten it. The man kept consulting his piece of paper. It was clear that he had no idea where he was. He was lost, I told myself, and with him the van, which was so expensive-looking that it might have contained chinchilla furs or imported chocolates or dresses from Paris instead of merely ice, dry ice, and ice cubes. He stared toward Seventh Avenue, where the lights of the Latin Quarter and Playland were dead in the daylight, and he took a few steps in that direction, and then he returned to the van and stood beside it again. Then he looked toward Sixth, which was almost the whole length of the block away from him, and he glanced down at his paper, and he looked at Sixth again, and thought a minute, and walked away in the direction of Sixth and out of my sight.

The van sat there, undefended but not quite deserted; the thin, smudged face of a cat peered out from underneath it, looking to see if it was safe to cross the street. It was safe — no cars coming — and she hurried across and into the parking lot on her way to make one of her daily inspections of the garbage cans that stand at the foot of the building I was in and behind the little buildings that had their backs to me. The little cat settles down in front of what used to be Zucca's door every morning at daybreak and begins to wait there for somebody to give her breakfast. Next to Zucca's old place is Puerto Sagua, and next to that is Tony's Pizzeria. Now the swinging doors of the pizzeria flew open and a very large and lordly man came out. He had light red hair, his shirtsleeves were turned back, he had a cigarette in the corner of his mouth, and he was carrying some business papers, which he folded as he walked. He went around the van, opened the door, stepped up and in, and sat down and started the engine and sped away, still with the cigarette in the corner of his mouth. He was so sure of himself that he didn't even bother to put his hand on the door beside him to see if it was closed tight. It was his door, and it knew its job, just as he knew his job. The doors of the pizzeria were still shivering after his triumphant exit, and I wondered what operatic scene of rage or sorrow or mirth might be taking place in there now by the cash register. As for the lost man, I think he may have been on his way to apply for a job. If he was, I hope he got it, if it was a job he wanted.

AUGUST 7, 1965

Little Birds in Torture

I WANTED one of those plain glass orange squeezers that generally cost about twenty-nine cents, and the nearest place I could think of where I could be sure of finding one was an enormous five-and-ten-cent store in midtown, so I went there, and down into the basement, where the kitchen things are. The basement is arranged in the usual, practical five-and-ten-cent-store fashion, with long counters separated by aisles, and when you walk about there you notice that there are no windows, and that the ceiling seems low and the lights glare, and you can imagine that you are in a very busy all-night bazaar, where everyone is hurrying to get what he wants and get away out of that heavy subterranean air. It is a feverish, nervous place. I found the orange squeezer without much trouble, and while I was waiting for change I glanced across at the bird department, one counter away from me, against the wall. I generally manage to forget those birds, but the orange squeezer had brought me too close to them, and I went over and looked into the cages. Three cages held birds. There was quite a large cage with a few parakeets, a small cage with three tiny birds in chalky browns and grays, and an equally small cage crowded with tiny bright-colored birds, orange and black and yellow and red. I counted them, and there were fourteen, in a cage meant for one or two, and when I had finished counting I saw that they had no water. There was some question about who was in charge of the birds, but finally she came, and I saw their minute water container filled, and then I left. The sign near them said IMPORTED FINCHES, and I wondered what country they had been brought from. I keep trying to think about the ordinary city birds, the pigeons and sparrows and so on, that fly around freely and seem able to find a living, but I cannot get those tortured finches out of my mind. The next time I want an orange squeezer, I will do my best to remember where the nearest hardware store is. A short walk out of my way seems a small price to pay for the privilege of avoiding reality.

NOVEMBER 24, 1962

A Young Lady with a Lap

SATURDAY nights begin very quietly in New York City in the summertime. Even Broadway cannot hurry the darkness those big lights need, and Broadway must have the big lights to transform her from ramshackle and dusty into what she really is: an island of unimaginable pleasures, where the forbidden fruit is within reach at last — still out of sight but within reach, somewhere here, very close now. There is something on Broadway that is not to be found at home, and everyone who walks along the great street begins to look for it. No other place is so blatant and secret, so empty and alive, so unreal and familiar, so private and noisy. To walk along Broadway is like being a ticket in a lottery — a ticket in a glass barrel, being tossed about with all the other tickets. There are eyes everywhere. I watched the crowd that roamed along there last night, moving through the lonely light that comes after sunset, during the hour when the sky is vacant and the moon is still powerless. High in the fading sky, the big lights glimmered faintly, creating an architectural mirage that was like the reflection of another city — the New York no one has ever found, perhaps. The Broadway crowd was eager but disheveled; it looked like the end of a long day's sightseeing. All the smart people were away for the weekend or waiting on their own side of town for curtain time. As I came near the Latin Quarter, a girl appeared in the crowd, walking alone. She wore a tight white crêpe dress, much whiter than flesh, and she had a small, fluffy white mink stole around her shoulders and her bosom. She was very slim, and she walked like two snakes, while her hemline slithered about her knees. She was much too clever to wear a very short dress. She showed her knees, and left the rest to her audience, to us — to all of us. We all looked. Her dress was more than very tight. It was extremely tight. Nobody looked at her knees. Everybody looked at her lap. Her hair was gold and it glittered, and so did her slippers, which were of transparent plastic edged with gold. She carried a small handbag, also of transparent plastic edged with gold, but it contained nothing except a gold lipstick, which rolled about like dice. I thought at first she must have some money tucked away in the tops of her stockings or somewhere, but as far as I could make out she had nothing at all on under her dress. We all stared at her, in our different ways, and from our attention she drew the air of indifference that made her a star. She cast swift glances right and left to show us how she despised us all, and then she vanished, leaving us with nothing to look at except ourselves. On the east side of Seventh Avenue, the Metropole Café was going full blast, as it does almost all day and almost all night. They have curtained off the side windows of the Metropole, so you have to stand up near the glass doors if you want to get a free glimpse of the almost naked girls dancing on the shelf behind the bar, but even so there is always a fascinated crowd around there, with a policeman saying sensible things like "Move along now." Not far from the Metropole, on the corner of Forty-ninth, a very spacious cigar store sells the cigarettes and cigars of all nations, but if you ask for a package of plain American cigarettes they show you where the machine is. Forty-ninth in that block between Seventh and Sixth Avenues is one of the several narrow little side streets that revel in the overflow from Broadway. It is a tumble-down block, lined with bars and small restaurants, and last night sailors in white suits were swarming like bees around the doors of all the bars, trying to decide which one looked the gayest, or the rowdiest, or the cheapest — or, at any rate, trying to decide which one they wanted to go into. I walked along to Le Steak de Paris, a French restaurant that has been in the same house, No. 121, for twenty-five years. Last night it was quiet there — very quiet in comparison with the excited street outside. There was a row of decorous customers at the bar, but the tables in the front room were all empty, and in the back room only one table was occupied — by a neat, dark young man, who sat alone with his back to the wall. He was a lucky man, dining peacefully in a nice French restaurant so close to Broadway that all he had to do was step outside the door but so quiet that he had all the attention in the house. He was eating *scallopines de veau en crème,* and there was a half bottle of wine on his table. When he wasn't watching the people at the bar, he was reading a paperback book — something by Simenon. In the doorway leading to the back room, Francine, the waitress, and Jo, the waiter, both from Brittany, stood waiting in a serenity that had in it neither patience nor impatience. It was early yet, still almost as light as day. The regular customers would begin to drift in soon. I went on to Sixth Avenue. Schrafft's was full of people eating their dinner at the counter. You don't have to be a customer to know what's going on in that Schrafft's. The street walls are made mostly of glass. The crowd on Sixth was more desultory than the crowd on Broadway, as it always is — more desultory and more inward-thinking. Sixth Avenue is simply the thoroughfare that lies between Fifth and Seventh. There was room and need for a street there, so they put one there and called it Sixth. People walk on Sixth Avenue because they are leaving someplace or going someplace, but as a promenade it is no man's land. I kept thinking about the girl in the mink stole. She must have had a pocket in the stole, where she kept some money. In that case, why not put the lipstick in the pocket and leave the handbag at home? She must have had a very well considered reason for carrying the handbag, and it would have to be a better reason than that the handbag matched the shoes. I wish I knew what her reason was. And then, of course, there may not have been a pocket in the stole.

SEPTEMBER 3, 1966

The Morning After

I WOKE up shortly before six o'clock this morning, Sunday, to the screaming of fire sirens that came very close to my hotel and then stopped, and after they stopped

there were a few loud shouts, and then the crash of breaking glass, all very familiar sounds in this crowded Broadway side street of old hotels and rooming houses and
bars and restaurants and dry cleaning places. There always
seems to be a little fire starting up around here. I got up
and went to the windows, and around the corner of the
front wing of the hotel, through the high narrow space
that separates it from its neighbor hotel, I could see sheets
of smoke blowing along the street toward Sixth Avenue,
but the smoke was white, not black, and it soon turned
transparent, showing no danger, and after watching a few
minutes I went back to sleep for another hour. The fire
had broken out half a block away, in the basement under a
haberdashery store, and later in the morning I walked
along Forty-ninth Street to inspect the damage. It was
about ten-thirty or so, the day was bright, and there were a
good many weekend tourists about, strolling aimlessly,
obviously wondering what you do in New York on a Sunday to kill time before you start back home again. As I
passed the shiny clean Salvation Army headquarters,
seven or eight workers, men and women, all in uniform
and all looking good-humored and energetic, came out
and we walked more or less together to the corner. The
unlucky haberdashery is on the corner of Seventh Avenue
and Forty-ninth Street, on the north corner, and I stood
on the south corner and looked. The store was wrecked, all
the big plate-glass windows shattered, and men in green
uniforms were sweeping up the broken glass. The curb
was lined with heaps of debris, wet and blackened, wood

and tin and cloth, and inside the store you could see rows
and rows of shirts still arranged in tidy piles on their
shelves and all the shirts looked spoiled. It would be a big
fire sale. The sidewalk around the derelict store was railed
and roped off, and people passing stopped for a minute to
look at the mess and watch the men in shirtsleeves who
were trying to clean it up. The men, evidently men em-
ployed in the store, were picking up — little frames with
shirts still stretched across them, a pink plastic foot that
had lost the sock it displayed yesterday, woebegone remnants, scorched and soaked — and dropping everything
into large brown cartons that had FRAGILE printed on their
sides. There were policemen about. You would be amazed
to see how neatly the firemen had cut off the fire and
confined it to its source. The haberdasher's is quite a big
place, but the corner it occupies represents only a tiny part
of that huge building, and although the shop was all broken and blackened, the restaurant windows directly above
and to the side of it were untouched and showed no effect
at all, even of smoke. Behind me I heard familiar music
and I turned to see that my companions from the Salvation Army had all lined up on my corner. One of them, an
elderly lady, stepped forward, out of the line, and began to
speak. She had a clear, high, elocutionary voice that carried a good distance. She announced that they were going
to sing a hymn to life and beauty, and then she stepped
back into the line and they all began to sing in brave,
tuneless voices. Right beside me I heard a man saying

"Where is Broadway?" and I looked quickly to find the question was addressed not to me but to three nice-looking, carefully dressed people, a man and two women, and the three began immediately to stare helpfully around in all directions, looking for Broadway, while the man who had asked the question looked interestedly into their faces and repeated his question. "Where is Broadway?" he said again. I almost spoke up, to tell him he was practically standing on Broadway, but then I took a good look at him. He was a big man, and he stooped a little, and he wore no jacket and no tie and the cuffs of his shirt were flapping up. His large pink face, which he had not shaved, wore an expression that was benign, but that might turn sardonic, and I looked quickly back to the fire. There is no telling what a man with that expression on his face might say next. Around the burnt store two cheerful young policemen were arranging those yellow wooden barricades they put up to protect areas of importance or disaster, and one of the men filling the cartons straightened up and looked at them and stretched his back and looked in discouragement at his filthy hands and went back to his miserable job. A man I recognized from my hotel came and stood near me. He said, "It was some fire." I said I was sorry for the men who had been called in on their day off to do all that clearing up. "And that's nothing to the inventory," my friend said. "From now on, inventory, inventory, everything is inventory. Every shirt, every tie, every button. Everything must be accounted for." And he crossed the

street to get a better look. The Salvation Army had
stopped singing, and I turned to see that one of the
younger women had stepped forward and was talking, and
I also saw the man who had been looking for Broadway.
He was standing at the end of the line of uniforms with a
hymn book in his hands, and his face as he listened to the
girl was attentive and respectful but still bland with the
ability he had to change faces. I noticed then that he wore
white canvas shoes. Two women in flowered dresses
walked past me, one of them carrying a small brown
puppy that looked much too young to have left its mother.
They came from Broadway, talking away, and they paid no
attention to the burnt-out store or to the Salvation Army
or to anything except their own conversation. They were
neighborhood people, out for a stroll, going toward Fifth,
and the little dog, not knowing he was safe, stared agitat-
edly about him as if he were blind. The Salvation Army
meeting was coming to an end. The elderly lady who had
spoken first stepped forward and spoke again. "If you are
a visitor in town, " she cried, "do not think only about
pleasure." I started back along Forty-ninth Street. The
gypsy ladies had not yet appeared in the doorway of their
ornate parlor, which is five steps up from the street, but
next door to them the movie theater with the scandalous
posters outside seemed open and ready for business. The
Salvation Army members walked back to their headquarters, all of them going at a smart pace but going separately,
straggling apart, and the unshaven man, without his hymn

book, followed close behind them. He limped very badly.
His feet must have been in terrible shape.

                                                    1969

The Two Protesters

AT a quarter to one this morning, I went into the
delicatessen in my hotel building to buy cigarettes.
The hotel and delicatessen are on West Forty-ninth Street
near Seventh Avenue, and at that hour of the morning the
block is very busy; it is lined on both sides with bars and
small restaurants and other night places, and there is noise
of a loud musical kind from most of the doorways, and
confusion on the street, with visitors to the Broadway area
wandering around wondering where they will get the best
value for their money. At my end of the block, the buildings go up very high, making the sudden New York darkness — no sky — but the sidewalk lies in a glare of hard,
different-colored artificial lights, and it is all very rowdy
and lonely. In the delicatessen, which is a high-ceilinged,
cluttered cave carved out of the front of my hotel, there
were a man and a woman ahead of me making up their
minds about sandwiches — what kind of sandwiches they
would buy, and on what kind of bread. They were staying
in a big hotel across the street, and they wanted to take the
sandwiches and some beer back to their room and have a

private supper together. I had got out of a taxi and walked straight into the delicatessen without noticing anything out of the way, but as I stood waiting, and watching the counterman make the sandwiches, I began to hear the voice of a man howling in the street outside. It wasn't a desperate howling, as though he were crying for help, and it wasn't a silly, playful howling; it was a determined, controlled sound, spaced out, as though he were saying words. At the same time, there was a good deal of laughter going on — such unrepressed, jolly laughter that I thought there must be a party of revelers out there and that one of them had found a way to amuse the rest and keep their attention. I didn't look out, but when I left the delicatessen, with my cigarettes, the noise was still going on. It was very warm (for spring), and in front of a gypsy tea-leaf-reading parlor across the narrow street two young sailors were dancing about, playing the clown for two dark girls sitting inside, who had a small child with them. But the sailors weren't howling, I could see that, and then, when I turned to the entrance of my hotel, I saw the man, standing alone about fifteen feet away from me. He was an astonishingly tall, thin man in a blue suit, and he had his head and shoulders thrown violently back. His face was turned up to the sky. He had only one leg, and his crutches, which were like stilts, were both braced in front of him so that they slanted back as he did. He was at a dangerous angle, as if he were falling slowly backward, but he did not fall, although it seemed that he might be thrown with each new effort he took to send his voice up. The people near him, all scattered, were smiling, but across the street a group of men and women were convulsed with laughter as they watched him. He paid no attention to anyone. All those about him seemed to be standing on solid ground while he was at the Edge, but although he was making no sense, he seemed to be making a good deal more sense than those who were laughing at him, and they, of normal height and standing on two legs, seemed more grotesque than he. I suppose some of the people were laughing because they were uneasy; certainly the crowd across the street thought it was being entertained, but there must have been a few who wished, as I did, that he would vanish. I don't know.

I went on up to the place I have in the hotel. I was thinking about another man I had seen making himself public, but that had been on a bright Friday afternoon last May, and the crowd that gathered to watch had looked sadly at him. It was a mournful gathering in the afternoon sunlight. What that man had done was to smash the large plate-glass window on the Sixth Avenue side of the Forty-ninth Street Schrafft's, which is a long, narrow corner restaurant with no tables, only a counter. He was a very small man, about five feet one, and he was wearing a round, muffin-shaped cap with a peak, very like a seaman's cap, and a neat black suit and striped shirt, and he was carrying a large bunch of long-stemmed red roses loosely wrapped in pink-and-white-striped paper. A big, elderly policeman, who looked unhappy, was guarding him beside the window, which was so thoroughly shattered that there was no glass to be seen except on the sidewalk, where two counterboys with brooms were cheerfully sweeping up. The cheer they showed was all the cheer there was. Inside the window was the wreckage of the glass shelves and of the food they had displayed — cakes and buns and jars of butterscotch and fudge sauce — and it was all being cleared up by young girls who looked apprehensive. The policeman looked downcast, and everybody in the crowd looked downcast, except one well-dressed young man, who kept sneaking glances right and left into the faces nearest to him and half smiling, as though he had a secret and unpleasant understanding of what had happened. The little captive looked interested and obedient, not ashamed or frightened or angry. He was mute. I don't know why he had broken the window or what he had broken it with. At the time of the crash, I had been sitting at the end of the counter, far away from the window, and by the time I had made up my mind to go outside, the discussions were over and there was nothing going on except waiting, with the policeman in charge. I went off without delay. What was strange on that corner that afternoon was the expression of the crowd. There was not one face that looked indifferent or amused. You do not often see a street crowd thinking, or appearing to think.

The only thing I have left to say about the two protesters, or protestants, is that one of the men was black and one was white.

APRIL 25, 1964

Lost Overtures

E ARLY the other evening, I was sitting in a restaurant on lower Fifth Avenue that has peach-colored walls and a softly lighted mirror running the length of the bar, when a striking red-haired lady in a black dress with pearls who was sitting by herself at a table not far from mine stood up and walked to a corner table where a nice-looking man was sitting alone reading his evening paper while he waited for someone to come and take his order. He was a careful, orderly man — he had already folded his newspaper up small, so that he could read it and at the same time eat his dinner. The lady bent over this man and said something to him, and he glanced up and then got up immediately, looking very pleased and confused, and collected his briefcase and followed her back to her table. He was still clutching his newspaper. She sat down, but at the last moment, when he was almost in his chair, he hesitated and began looking around him and behind him. "Are you sure you're alone?" he asked. "Of course I'm alone," she replied. "Stop asking me if I'm alone." He sat down, and she picked up her drink and started gazing at him possessively. She looked possessive but very good-humored. They were just beginning to talk when the headwaiter, a big, dignified man, appeared from a distant corner of the restaurant and saw the change that had been made in his seating arrangements. He walked swiftly to where the lady sat with her flattered captive, who had settled back and seemed about to relax. "Sir," said the headwaiter, "please go back to your own table." The man (*everything* was happening to *him*) jumped up, gathering his briefcase and his newspaper to his chest, and scurried to his corner table, and picked up the menu and held it in front of his cowardly face. The lady was annoyed. "Just who do you think you are?" she said to the headwaiter. "Lady," said the headwaiter, "do me a favor. Please go home." "Don't talk to me like that," she said. "Who do you think you are? Don't you talk to me like I was dirt." "Lady," said the headwaiter, "please don't tell *me* that I am talking to *you* like you were dirt." Unfortunately, I had already paid my check and put on my gloves, and I hadn't the nerve to just sit there watching, so I had to leave without hearing the rest of the repartee.

Two evenings later I was in Le Steak de Paris on West Forty-ninth Street. It was peaceful there — a warm, rainy evening. I had worked my way through *Time,* back to front, and I was starting in on *Newsweek* when someone came and stood beside me. I looked up, and it was a very tall, solemn, scholarly-looking young man who had made a good deal of fuss over his briefcase when he came into the restaurant. He had given his hat to the checkroom girl, but he had taken his briefcase to the bar with him after explaining to her that he was afraid something might happen to it. Then, when he sat at the bar — it is a very small restaurant, everything in one room — he had balanced the briefcase on his feet for a while, which meant that he had to keep reaching down to set it straight. Finally, he had gone back and given it to the checkroom girl, and watched while she put it away on a high shelf. That had all happened some time before. Now he stood by my table and looked gloomily at me and said, "I don't mean to insult you." Then he said, "I want to know if you will have a drink with me." I said, "No, thank you. I am waiting for somebody." I was sitting at a table for one. "You are waiting for somebody," he said, and he went back to his place at the bar. Ten or fifteen minutes later, two ladies in small, serviceable hats came in and sat down at the table next to me. They spoke French. One of them was French, or spoke like a Frenchwoman, and the other was speaking some French she had learned, using only whole sentences, and they both had loud, confident voices. The scholarly man got off his stool and came over to them. "I don't mean to insult you," he said. They stared up at him. He began to smile, and then he beamed at them. *"Parlez-vous Berlitz?"* he said. M. Raymond, who had been gazing into the cash register, hurried over and took him by the elbow and began to tow him back to the bar. "Monsieur," M. Raymond said, "you don't know those people. Please, Monsieur, *s'il vous plaît.*" "I didn't mean to insult anybody," the man said, but he allowed himself to be placed back at the bar, where he sat guarding his drink with both elbows and looking resentful.

The lesson to be learned from these two encounters is that if everybody in the city were sorted out and set going in the right direction, New York would soon be a very quiet place.

JULY 4, 1964

The Man Who Combed His Hair

THERE IS a man around this neighborhood who is always combing his hair. Once I saw him borrow a comb from a very small shoeshine boy. Then, while he combed his hair, combing it with one hand and smoothing it with the other, he bent and looked into the child's face as though the little face were a mirror — only a mirror, and nothing more than that. The boy stood and looked up at him, waiting to get his comb back. I was in my hotel room, looking down into the street and watching the two of them. I am eight floors up in one of those old hotels that line the shabby side streets off Broadway in midtown, and it was a hot Sunday morning about nine o'clock. The street had been deserted until the shoeshine boy and the man who combs his hair came into view, walking with four older and taller shoeshine boys, all carrying their boxes of brushes and polish. When the man borrowed the comb, he stopped and stood still, and so did the small boy whose face became a mirror, but the others went on and out of sight, walking toward Broadway. When the man had finished — when he seemed satisfied with his appearance, whatever he thought that was — he gave the comb back to the child, who took it and put it in the breast pocket of his shirt, and then the two walked on un-til, I suppose, they caught up with their companions. It wasn't the first time I had seen that man. The first time I had seen him, he had been at exactly the same point on the block as when he stood looking down into the child's face, but he had been five flights up, walking on the roof of one of the few little houses that still stand together there, holding their own against the gigantic new buildings that have risen up around them. The little houses are no longer dwellings where ordinary families live. There are restaurants or small shops on their street floors, and above there are other shops — a theatrical costumer's or a dress or record shop — or there are studios or offices or a few apartments. The house where the man was walking on the roof has a steak restaurant on the street floor and, above, studios for musicians to practice in. The studios have long, uncurtained windows. One of the windows shows a blue light, and sometimes late at night the blue light betrays the source of some very blue music. The saxophonist who plays in there must be very sad and very slow to learn. Even so, I like to hear him — his mistakes and his hesitations and his false starts. It is like hearing music in the street — very comforting, or perhaps I mean comfortable. But on the morning I am thinking of there was no music and no blue light. The day had only begun. The windows of all the houses were blank and the street was empty. It was a hot morning after a scorching night. There had been no dawn — the darkness had merely faded away, showing the city to be gray, worn, and sleepless. The sky was very high and colorless. It was not fair. The sky promised nothing — no soft rain, no relief from the heat — but still it was beautiful up there. A few pigeons pecked in the de-

serted parking lot under my windows, and others flew
hopefully about, but apart from the pigeons there was no
life to be seen except on the roof, where the man who
combs his hair was walking with some men who were
unsteadily following another man, who was carrying a
bottle that looked as if it contained wine. He was carrying it at about shoulder height and at arm's length in front
of him, as though it might show him the way, like a
lantern. There were five men altogether, going single file,
and they had more difficulty than you might think in their
little passage around the roof. Things kept getting in their
way — things on the roof. All the low roofs around there
seem to have been patched and furnished with wreckage
swept in from the sea; useful bits of freighters and tankers
and steamers, funnels and pipes and cabins, all of them
blackened and valuable shapes, together with skylights of
different sizes and great, sprawling air-conditioning units,
strewed the path of the five wandering men, who looked
so unsubstantial that a breath of wind might blow them
away. There was no wind, no air at all. The men weaved
around and about, following their restless leader, and the
last man combed his hair. He wore the same clothes that
he has worn every time I have seen him — a green plaid
Eisenhower jacket and crumpled cotton trousers of a light
color — and as he combed and smoothed his hair, keeping his elbows well out, he ducked his head and shoulders
to the right and to the left and seemed to find himself
reflected in the unsteady back of the man in front of him.
He bent forward and inclined his head and turned from

side to side as though he were peering at himself in a mountain pool in strong sunshine. He stepped along easily and he seemed to be enjoying himself there on the roof in the discouraged daylight. The last time I saw him, I was walking along Seventh Avenue near the Metropole jazz place, just around the corner from where I live. He was standing outside one of the glittery gift shops there, talking to a man who was selling sunglasses. The salesman was wearing a pair of his own sunglasses. At least he was wearing sunglasses. I saw the man who combs his hair walk up to the sunglasses man and greet him. The sunglasses man returned the greeting, and as soon as they began to talk, the man who combs his hair took out his comb and started, as usual, combing his hair and smoothing it and leaning forward for a better look, peering first into his friend's right sunglass and then into his left one. He bobbed his head from side to side and combed and smoothed and talked and watched his face sliding around in the dark glass. He was wearing the same clothes as always — the plaid Eisenhower jacket and the crumpled trousers — and I saw, seeing him close up for the first time, that he was about thirty-five and tired-looking but amiable. I have not seen him for a while now, and I would just as soon not see him again. I know we are all only reminders of one another, but I don't want him to walk up to me and look into my face as though I were a mirror. What I would like even less would be to look into his face and see myself hiding there.

SEPTEMBER 5, 1964

The Good Adano

DURING the recent heat wave, all air ceased to flow through the streets of New York City. There was no air moving between the buildings, and what air had been trapped here stood still and began to thicken. There was nothing to breathe except heavy displeasure. Every time I walked into an air-conditioned restaurant, I felt very humble and thankful and anxious to sit down and start being good. I wasn't the only one. On the afternoon of the dreadful third of July (it was a Sunday), I was in the Adano Restaurant, on West Forty-eighth Street. I was happy. It seemed a miracle that the one restaurant in New York where I really wanted to be should not only be open on a Sunday, when so many places are closed, but be open on the Sunday of the longest summer weekend, and on a weekend so uneasy with the heat that even Manhattan's towering skyline appeared to waver under the fixed abyss that shimmered up there where Heaven used to be. At the Adano, the air-conditioning machine was producing ocean breezes. In this chaotic Broadway neighborhood, the Adano has always been an oasis of order and good manners and beautiful food, but that Sunday it seemed to have drifted here from another, more silent region. The restaurant is a wide oblong, with a low ceiling, lighted by star-shaped lamps of dull-yellow glass. The walls are decorated with large, placid still lifes and views of Italian scenery, except for the rear wall, which has mirrors that carry the room into the far distance. The tables are plain and

plainly set, with well-worn silver and with white linen
napkins folded to stand up in smart points. Empty as it
was, and with everything polished and shining, the restaurant looked like a dining room on a small, tidy ship. I was
sitting at the front, in one of three half-moon-shaped
booths near the street door. I faced the bar, and in the
mirror behind the shelves of bottles I saw the reflection of
grapes and apples in the rich still life on the wall behind
me and above my head. And through the glass panels of
the doorway I could see the street, where the rose-red
Adano awning cast a curious shadow on the burning sidewalk. Very few people passed. Once in a while, a wilted
figure in summer undress climbed the sweaty steps that
lead to the ticket and information bureau of the Blue Line
Sightseeing Bus Tours, which is on the first floor of a poor
old brownstone across the street. The old house is one of
three that still stand together there, but the two others
have had their faces flattened out. The house where the
Blue Line people are has aged as naturally and as recog-
nizably as a human being might do. It is the same as it
always was, except that too many years have passed and
life has not improved for it. There is a bar in the basement,
but it was closed that Sunday. A man walked into the
Adano suddenly and then hesitated just inside the door,
looking around him. He was a very nice-looking, pale,
thin man of about fifty, with not much hair, and he was
politely dressed in a dark blue summer suit, a snowy white
shirt, and a neat dark tie with dots on it. When he spoke,
he had a pleasant, squeaky voice. I am sure he was a

stranger in the city. He had an out-of-town look about
him. I think he had rashly left his nice air-conditioned
hotel in the hope of finding a real New York place, a place
with atmosphere, where he would get something of the
feeling of the city, and I think he must have wandered
about for a while before he happened into the Adano. He
must have been getting a bit frantic, not wanting to continue in the heat and loneliness, and not wanting to go
back to the boredom of a long afternoon in the nice hotel
that is almost certainly exactly like all nice hotels in big
cities. Wandering around alone like that in New York City
on a Sunday is no good at all. He stood there looking at
me and looking at the bartender and looking beyond us at
the calm room, and at last he called out to the bartender,
"Are you open?" "Yes, we are open," the bartender said
benignly. He was polishing a glass. The stranger walked
over to the bar and sat up on a stool and put his hands on
the counter. "Could I just sit here and have a beer, please?"
he asked. He sounded just the way I felt — on his best
behavior. It was a day to smile eagerly back at Good
Fortune if she happened to look your way, a day to say
please and thank you and to watch your p's and q's and to
look out for ladders and to watch yourself crossing streets,
and so on — the heat had roused superstitious dreams and
made us careful. People began coming into the Adano. A
family party, mother and father and three young children,
walked in and went straight to a table at the back. The
mother and father immediately began reading the menu
aloud, and the children all sat forward and listened as

intently as though they were at a story hour. Then two women walked in — tall, strong, opulently shaped girls of about thirty who looked as though they must be in show business. Their walk was sedate, as it well might be, because their dresses did all the work — slinky, skintight, slithering dresses that recalled the body of Circe, the gestures of Salome, and the intentions of Aphrodite. One dress was of white lamé sewn all over with tiny pearls and brilliants, and the other was of shiny baby-pink cotton striped up and down in thin lines with pink glass bugle beads. Each of the girls carried a cloudy gray mink stole and long gloves and a little fat handbag, and each of them, as she sat down, swept her right hand underneath herself to make sure her dress did not wrinkle, while her eyes went swiftly about the restaurant in a wary, commanding glance that took in everything there was to see. Then, without speaking to each other, the two girls examined the menu, and they ordered at once — food only, nothing to drink — and when the food began arriving they ate steadily. They emptied big plates of hot soup, plates piled with meat and vegetables, and plates with heaps of salad, and they ate a lot of crusty Adano bread with butter, and when all that was gone they had coffee — American coffee — and a slice each of glistening rum cake. While they were eating, they talked a bit — not much — but they never smiled, and as I watched them I began to be deeply fascinated by them, because their closed faces and their positive, concentrated gestures excluded every single thing in the world except themselves. Outside herself and what contributed to her, nothing existed for either of them. They were all flesh and color and movement, and yet they were like stone monuments whose eating time had come and who would, when they had finished eating, go back to being monuments. I watched them and I wondered at them, because I thought them untroubled by every emotion except anger, and free of all sensations except the sensations of satisfaction. They made no delay over their dinner, and when they had finished they paid their check and stood up and collected their belongings and walked out with the hypnotic sedateness with which they had come in. I turned my head to watch them go, and so did the stranger at the bar, and then he went back to admiring the restaurant he had discovered, and he seemed like the man at the ship's bar just after sailing time who still cannot believe that he has made it — that he is on board, at sea, and it is all as he imagined it. As much as anybody in New York that Sunday, the man at the bar of the Adano found himself where he had dreamed of being.

AUGUST 6, 1966

A Busload of Scolds

MANY of those huge buses that bring people from out of town into the city for a few hours' visit seem to deposit their passengers on the side streets off

Sixth Avenue near Radio City. One Saturday afternoon recently, I was walking past one of those parked buses when I found myself caught in the middle of a crowd of indignant women in little summer hats who were scolding the driver because he had not brought them to the spot where they had expected to be. They had been told, or they had understood, that their ride would end at a point along the river where they could board the boat that goes around Manhattan, and instead they were on the corner of Forty-ninth Street and Sixth Avenue, and by the time they found their own way over to the river, they said, the boat would have left. The driver, who looked tortured, was trying to gain time for himself by carefully examining every one of the tickets that were being waved in his face, and I pushed my way out of the crowd without waiting to hear what explanation he would find for his passengers. All the same, I could not help smiling to think how re-spectfully all those women must have sat behind him as he drove them in — you know how omnipotent those long-distance drivers look, enthroned alone up high in their front place — and how quickly they had turned on him when they discovered that instead of shepherding them he had led them astray, and was going to have to leave them astray, wandering in the city, and was going to have to force himself to climb back up there in front of them later on and listen to their complaints and recriminations dur-ing the long drive home. I was sorry for them all, but I thought they ought to be congratulating themselves on the coolness of the day. I had been thinking about the pleasures of cool weather as I walked up Sixth, which was full of travelers who had come to New York for the day or for the weekend, all of them walking steadily along as though they had been told that they had the whole length of the island to go before they found the way out, or the road home, or the sight they had come to see. The day was not truly cool — there was heat somewhere in the air and no mistaking that it was midsummer — but it was nice out.

After leaving the bus driver and his problems, I walked into Le Steak de Paris, which was where I had been headed for, and I observed with approval that they had noted the temperature of the day and had left the air-conditioning off and the door open. I usually sit at a small table facing the bar, but it was occupied, and I walked back and sat down to an unfamiliar view; instead of looking at the bar, with its mirrors and clocks and bottles and distillery souvenirs, I was looking along the whole length of the bar and past it at the big front restaurant window and at the street outside. Out there were some more of the people I had seen walking along Sixth Avenue; now they were going to and from Broadway. The window encloses the whole square front of the restaurant, but it is curtained across the top and at the sides, so that only a small rectangle of glass is left uncovered, above a tall old radiator that hides the hips and legs of the bodies walking by outside. I watched the crowd, and once I saw two round heads covered with light fuzz go bobbing past, and I knew that two small boys had just gone by. Inside, the restaurant was quiet — too quiet for the proprietor, who had taken charge of the bar himself for the slow afternoon and stood bowed moodily over his newspaper nearly all the time I was there. The restaurant is cheerful, with a hammered-tin ceiling and an assortment of wallpapers — red brick wallpaper, gray brick wallpaper, gay Parisian wallpaper — on different walls. Over the corner where the coat-check girl stands in wintertime there is a small square canopy, striped in brown and white. In the summertime, since there are fewer customers and no coats, the check girl goes away somewhere. When I had nearly finished lunch, a serious-looking young couple, a man and a girl, came in and sat up at the bar and ordered a drink. Then they changed their minds and carried their drinks to the table next to mine. As he was fitting her chair in under her, the man said, evidently continuing their conversation, "All right, if you must have a definition, I am a Socialist who is interested in lust." I was fascinated, but he sat down and his voice dropped with him, and I heard nothing more from him until their lunch had been served, and then he said, in a loud voice, as though he were astonished, "The potatoes are very good here." Another disappointing man, I thought, remembering the bus driver.

When I left the restaurant, the day had grown much darker. I was only a few steps along Sixth Avenue when some very large drops of rain fell loudly around me and on

me, and they were followed at once by a panicky downpour that cleared the sidewalks immediately. All the
people had squeezed themselves in against the buildings
and into doorways, and I started to squeeze myself into a
doorway, too, but I was already wet, so I thought I would
hurry over to Fifth Avenue and go along home. I got
soaked, but it didn't matter, I was going home, and as I
splashed along I thought once again of the bus driver, and
I hoped for his sake that all those angry ladies in their
summer clothes were safe under cover somewhere.

AUGUST 19, 1961

Movie Stars at Large

ONE night about ten years ago, very late at night, I
was sitting in the big, square bar of the Jumble
Shop when Jean Gabin walked in and sat down at a corner
table. Six years or so ago, I was having tea in Rosemarie de
Paris — the branch near Fifty-fourth Street — and found
that Marlene Dietrich was sitting at the table next to me. I
saw Judy Holliday strolling around the main floor of Lord
& Taylor one afternoon, maybe five years ago, and about
the same time, or perhaps a little earlier that year, I was
standing in an elevator that had stopped at the fourth floor
of Lord & Taylor, and Paulette Goddard stepped in, wearing a yellow dress. It must have been summertime, because
of the yellow dress. Judy Holliday was in heavy clothes. I

think I saw her in Lord & Taylor around Christmastime that year. As a matter of fact, I'm sure it was Christmastime, because I never walk around the main floor of any department store except at Christmastime, when I am looking for the kind of present you give to people who get scented sachets and Pullman slippers and feminine-looking billfolds and things like that. I like seeing movie stars as I go on my way around the city. I like recognizing them and knowing who they are and knowing that by just being where I am they make me invisible — a face in the crowd, another pair of staring eyes. I never jostle movie stars, or ask them for autographs, or try to snip locks of their hair, but I do stare. I feel that by recognizing them I have earned the right to stare, and I also feel that they do not really mind. It is different if you are not a movie star. One time I was mistaken for a movie star. Then, when the mistake had been cleared up, I was stared at for not being a movie star.

It was about fourteen years ago. I was sitting in the back room of the Minetta Tavern, and I had just finished dinner. I was waiting for my coffee. Suddenly a very small girl pressed herself against me and put an open autograph book on the table in front of me. I stared down at her and she stared up at me. We did not smile. Then a woman — her mother, I suppose — was over me.

The woman said, "Oh, Miss Astor, won't you give Rosalie your autograph? We've been watching you since we came in. I told her she'd see movie stars here."

I said, "But I am not Miss Astor."

The woman said, "Aren't you Mary Astor?"

I said, "No, of course not."

The woman said, "Well, you certainly do look like her."

I said to the little girl, "I'm terribly sorry. I can't write in your book."

The little girl put out her hand and laid it on the book.

The woman said, "Well, this is a disappointment. Can't you write your name anyway?" Then she said, very quickly, "Go ahead. Put 'Mary Astor.' Just write something. She won't know the difference."

I said, "No, I won't."

The woman grabbed the child and the autograph book angrily, and they went back to their table. I did not watch them go. I felt ashamed. After a while, I glanced across at their table. The child looked downcast and reproachful. She was watching me, and her autograph book dangled from her hands. The woman was staring at me. I thought she looked contemptuous. I felt even more ashamed. By walking into the Minetta Tavern when I was there, they had made me into an impostor. It was all my fault. I had been *anybody*, but now I was only *not somebody*. I left the restaurant in a hurry, without having any coffee.

Now I am coming to the point of my story. Since my return to the city after my long sojourn in the country, I have been staying around in different hotels in different neighborhoods searching for the place where I would really like to settle down. A while ago, I left the small hotel in the Village where I always used to stay, and moved to a

hotel on East Eighty-sixth Street, just across from Central
Park. One night — a Monday — I was going into the
hotel about nine o'clock when I noticed a commotion and
a lot of very bright lights, floodlights, on the corner of
Eighty-sixth and Fifth, directly across the street. I asked
the doorman what it was all about. "They're making some
movie," he said. I went into the hotel and asked the girl in
the elevator about the movie that was being made. "It's
Butterfield 8," she said. "Elizabeth Taylor is out there. And
Laurence Harvey."

It was threatening rain that night, and it was cold. I put
on a large felt hat and a raincoat, and I went down and out
and stood near the corner, watching the scene across the
street. The scene in and around the ring of floodlights and
cameras might have been roped or walled off, it was so
well protected by an army of policemen and other people
in authority, who were all kept busy easing the traffic out
of the way, and then easing it on its way, and encouraging
motorists to keep moving, and even persuading Fifth Avenue bus drivers into a pleasing show of docility. I stood
watching, to see what would happen. A few people stood
near me, and all the people walking their dogs paused to
watch a minute. It was really much too cold and windy to
stand still for long. Across the street, a tiny bright red car
was parked at the curb on the Fifth Avenue side of the big
apartment house that is on that corner. The car started
suddenly backward and shot around the corner and a short
way along Eighty-sixth, stopping just across from the en-

trance to my hotel. Elizabeth Taylor was at the wheel, and Laurence Harvey sat beside her. During the pause before she started the car again, Elizabeth Taylor glanced into the rear-view mirror and pushed idly at her dark hair, which was tousled, using her left hand. Laurence Harvey looked more closely into the rear-view mirror and, using both hands, combed his hair with a comb. At a signal that I did not notice, Miss Taylor shot the car forward and around the corner, and stopped it where it had originally been standing, just short of the apartment-house marquee. Mr. Harvey climbed unsteadily out of the car. He was wearing a topcoat. He staggered. A doorman in uniform rushed forward to support him. And so on. They went through their scene several times — many times — racing the car backward, stopping, and racing it forward again. It was really a very cold night. People kept coming to watch and then drifting away. At one point, a policeman came and put up a barrier in front of me. I looked around. I was the only person behind the barrier.

Now I have a dream. In my dream, it is about two o'clock in the morning and it is terribly cold. I am standing on the corner of Eighty-sixth and Fifth, and across the street, on the opposite corner, Greta Garbo is standing, surrounded by bright lights and big cameras. She is wearing an enormous fur hat that does not hide her splendid face. Where I am, it is dark. Across Fifth, the trees and grass and paths of Central Park have vanished into the night. There is no traffic of any kind. A policeman comes

and puts up a barrier in front of me. I look around. I am
alone. I am all the crowd there is. I *am* the crowd. I watch
Greta Garbo, and I roar like a crowd. My enthusiasm gets
the better of me and I howl. In a matter of minutes, I am a
mob. I press forward to get a better view of Miss Garbo,
and then I make a wild surge. The barrier comes down
with a crash. Policemen arrive and form a cordon to hold
me back. Two policemen get hold of the barrier and try to
stand it up while all the other policemen dig in their heels
and almost sit flat on the pavement in their determination
to keep me within limits. I begin to cheer. I am almost out
of control. I seem to be turning into a riot, but reinforce-
ments of police arrive and I quiet down. Soon I am back
behind the barrier. The policemen vanish. I continue to
watch Greta Garbo. Suddenly out of the shadows, Jean
Gabin appears. He is wearing the uniform of an officer in
the French Army in the war of 1914. M. Gabin says, "I've
been watching you for some time. Haven't we met someplace? I'm sure I know you." I say, "No, I don't think so."
He says, "You look very familiar. I'm sure I've seen you
before." I say, "I really don't think we've met, but I can tell
you one thing. I'm not Mary Astor. I don't even look like
her." M. Gabin replies, "Of course you're not Mary Astor.
There's no resemblance at all. How could there be? You
are invisible. Anybody can see that." He vanishes in the
shrouded direction of Central Park. I stand behind my
barrier and I continue to watch Greta Garbo.

So much for my dream, but, in fact, this is a wonderful

city. It is always giving me something to think about. Now I am thinking of Madison Avenue. The best bus ride in the city is along there, but tonight I think I will walk up Madison Avenue on my way home. I have never been invisible on Madison Avenue, but perhaps after the walk that I will take between ten minutes after six and twenty-five minutes to seven this evening there will be a different story to tell. Maybe Alec Guinness will be the one who will not see me.

DECEMBER 3, 1960

Faraway Places Near Here

I FIND the world noisy and intrusive in the summertime, and in the hot months I am always too conscious of the rooms I am living in and impatient with them, thinking of smothering, and for that reason, when the summer weather in New York City begins to reach its height, I am subject to powerful gusts of memory from other summers and other rooms in the different places in the city where I used to live. The summer on Sullivan Street was minute and hot and quiet, like the room I had, which measured about ten feet by twelve and had an enormous fireplace and no closet. Outside there was a little court with a fountain that never played, but the superintendent had a small boy, and the boy had a kitten, and they both enjoyed the court very much. On Hudson Street the room was larger and had an enormous fireplace and no kitchen, and the newspaper-and-soda shop on the ground floor next door had a jukebox that played "You Always Hurt the One You Love" all summer long with great beat and volume. I was on the third floor there, and the lady on the fourth floor got my check for the rent in her mailbox by mistake, and the landlady, who lived in suspicion on the first floor, kept asking me about the check, and finally I had to give her another check and stop payment on the first check, and then the fourth-floor tenant turned up with the original check and everybody seemed perfectly content that I was out the two dollars I had to give the bank for the stop payment. Next I moved to an enormous room on Tenth Street that had windows straight across the front, giving me a fine view of rooftops and sky, and I had a tiny fireplace that didn't work and two big closets. I was six flights up, and the ceiling was low and the flat roof above me was tarred, and the heat was intense, but all the same it was a lovely room, except when I was trying to pull myself together to go out. One Saturday night, I spent about two hours making myself presentable in the five-hundred-degree heat up in that room, and when I was ready to leave I was late and I ran down the six flights and did very well till I reached the top of the last flight, and there I tripped and tumbled head over heels down to the bottom. My arms were dirty and my white gloves were ruined and my hair was down and I thought of myself living in that hot, dirty house, and I sat on the floor in the hall and cried with rage.

The next stop I made was on Twenty-second Street, near Ninth Avenue, where I had two big rooms with a fireplace in each room and a real kitchen and the *use* of a garden. Outside, on Twenty-second Street, the people argued all day and then they argued all night, but more loudly at night because it was dark. When it rained, they got into the doorways to argue and then got out of the doorways to knock each other down. Over my head lived several young men who played "Come On-a My House" all evening every evening and all day long on Saturdays and Sundays. They had no rugs or anything on the floor, and when their phone rang they all made a rush for it and tackled it together. Their record player was powerful, and the sound pounded down through my ceiling until there was nothing in my head except that dreadful song. One Saturday afternoon, the owner of the building came to call. He owned it at long distance, through an agent and a manager, and his family had lived there once, and he walked into my apartment and took away the one thing that might have held me to the place — a magnificently ornate gilt mirror that filled the entire space between two windows. He said it was a family heirloom, and he and his abominable companion dragged it away, heavy and big as it was and much as I loved it, and put it in their station wagon and drove off with it. How I hated them. How I hoped it would break and give them seven years' bad luck.

From there I went to Ninth Street, near Fifth, where I had two nice rooms and a fireplace and a terrace that was surrounded in spring and summer by the tops of trees. Early one Sunday morning, my little cat climbed down from the terrace to the little bit of roof that jutted out below and sat up on a windowsill there staring in at the poodle who lived underneath me, and the poodle barked and woke his owners up and they became very objectionable, leaning out of their window and looking up at me and telling me my cat was a nuisance. I went downstairs and rescued her, and ever afterward when I passed them on the stairs I used to glare at them.

Another summer, I was living in the Hotel Earle in the Village, where I had two nice rooms with folding doors between them and windows taking in the breeze from three directions, when there was a breeze. That was the hottest summer I ever remember, but I do not remember what I heard or felt so much as what I saw. I used to leave the hotel about seven on weekdays to go to my office, which was air-conditioned, and one morning shortly after seven I was sitting at the counter of a drugstore that was then on the corner of Eighth Street and Fifth Avenue when a young black girl walked by outside wearing a yellow cotton dress. She was about seventeen, and she seemed to me to be newer than anything else in the city. Even at that hour the heat was stunning, but she looked newer than a daffodil. Her dress was triumphantly clean and starched, and I was sure she had ironed it herself, and

I felt rather ashamed, because I never iron anything anymore. She looked very resolute, walking to her work, and I
often think of her. Another morning I left the hotel late
— about nine-thirty or so — and as I made my way slowly
through the blinding heat along Waverly Place to Sixth I
saw a man approaching me who walked even more slowly
than I did, and he hesitated every few steps. His hands
were joined in front of him and he was carrying something
that took all his attention. He never raised his eyes from
what he was carrying in his hands. All the attention and
care he had left to give to anything he was giving to what
was in his hands, and he looked worn out and at the end of
his rope. He had on only a shirt and trousers and shoes, no
socks, and he was dirty and looked as though he had not
washed or shaved or slept for a week, and he also looked as
though he had no place to go where he could lie down and
rest. He came toward me, watching what was in his hands,
and I could hardly wait to see what he had that he treas-
ured so much, and when I was passing him I looked, and
there was a lump of ice melting in his hands. Then one
Sunday morning I was walking across Tenth to Fifth,
about noon, and, I have to say it again, the heat was past
description. On the other side of Tenth, wandering along
toward Sixth, I saw a man who used to hang around the
neighborhood there asking for money, and I thought I
would just go across and give him a quarter to relieve my
conscience, because I intended to have lunch in an air-
conditioned and expensive restaurant. I crossed the street,

which was deserted up and down, and when I got to where he had been he had vanished. I thought he might have fainted from hunger, and I looked, and there he was leaning halfway in along the back seat of a car going through some baskets and a suitcase that were there. I crept back to my own side of the street with my quarter in my hand, feeling terribly embarrassed to have seen him stealing and thanking heaven that he had not caught me prying. It seems to me that everything I feel about that summer and about every summer was contained in the thought I had then about that man, because the world was so distorted, dead in the heat, with nothing real and nothing unreal, that it seemed no more strange for him to steal than for me to climb up into a bus and be carried from one place to another place.

AUGUST 18, 1962

The Traveler

THERE is nothing like a short walk through this city to remind us of the accidental nature of our lives. Here it is a lovely Sunday in summer — the weather a miracle in itself — and it is a miracle I am alive to write this. I started my walk at Forty-fourth Street and Second Avenue, and the first thing that happened was that I almost got killed by an overexcited motorist who was taking

the corner much too fast. I would not have been alone in
my calamity. A young man and woman and their baby,
who were waiting along with me for the light to change,
would also have been run over. But we were all saved. The
man barely missed us, and screeched around without even
looking at us. We all walked across the avenue as though
nothing had happened, putting our common miracle behind us, along with the relief we did not want to acknowl-
edge. They continued with their lively baby along Forty-
fourth Street, but I had decided to do one block of Second
Avenue, which remains dismal in spite of the grandeur
that is rising up a block to the east along the river and
around the United Nations building. I turned off on
Forty-fifth Street, also dismal, and came out on Third
Avenue, which is no longer an avenue but a beautiful vista
as you look north. The removal of the El has revealed all of
the space and color and distance that Third Avenue used
to possess in secret, but I was walking step by step, and I
did not especially want to tackle a vista. I admired Third
Avenue for the length of a block, and then I went on over
to Lexington. I have no particular fondness for Lexington
Avenue. It is a useful place, lined with shops that are filled
with interesting things, but it is noisy and congested and I
think it nags for far more attention than it deserves. But
after my escape from sudden death I was well disposed to
whatever presented itself, and as I went along, looking
about me, I saw three tall, handsome people, two women
and a man, come out of a hotel and get into a limousine

that I was certain was taking them to Idlewild. They had
luggage and they were well dressed and they appeared to
be collected and in good humor, and I wondered where
they were going, and I envied them. I thought about Amsterdam and Marseille and Algiers, all places where I have
never been, and I wished I could turn myself into a transatlantic traveler for a few days, or even a week, and mas-
querade with luggage and a striped steamer rug in some
distant hotel lobby, and allow everybody to believe that I
had a very good and important reason for being there, and
that when I left I would have an urgent reason for leaving,
and that my next destination was fixed and depended on
plans that could not be changed. I wanted to be at the
mercy of strict arrangements for a little while, with a
timetable to guide me and tickets and a passport to explain
me, and to have a list of faraway hotel rooms that were
unknown to me now but that soon would be perfectly
familiar, because I would sleep in them. And my excuse
and explanation for being wherever I found myself would
always stand by me — my suitcase, recognizable in any
language. My suitcase would translate me to everybody's
satisfaction and especially to my own satisfaction. And I
would go to a city where the people spoke a language I did
not understand, so that I could listen as much as I liked
and still not eavesdrop. It is so nice to be able to listen to
voices without being delayed by what is being said. I
would go to Amsterdam. I might as well have been in
Amsterdam for all the attention I was giving to the city I

was walking in, and then I found myself at the Lexington
Avenue entrance of the Waldorf-Astoria Hotel.

With my vision of arrivals and departures and international travelers, I went into the Waldorf and began to
climb the stairs that lead to the main lobby. I thought I
would walk straight through the hotel to Park Avenue and
perhaps notice some transatlantic elegance on my way.
When I reached the lobby, I saw that it was crowded to its
last inch with groups of men and women delegates to
some convention. I have never in my life seen so many
people all so glad to see one another. They were having a
wonderful time. They were all smiling and shaking hands
and talking heartily. I hoped they would not begin to sing.
I got through the lobby as quickly as I could and hurried
out onto Park Avenue. I took a taxi to Le Steak de Paris,
on Forty-ninth between Sixth and Seventh, where I intended to have lunch. There were two men, not together,
at the bar in the little front room, but the tables were
empty. It was all Sunday quiet. I took the small table by
the window, and as I sat down a very young woman
walked slowly by outside, wheeling her baby. A very old,
bent woman walked beside her — the baby's grand-
mother, or more likely its great-grandmother. They must
live in the neighborhood, because the old woman, whose
dress was long and voluminous, wore an apron and slippers. She carried two handbags, her own and the girl's.
They had just come out for a minute, to give the baby its
Sunday airing. No one came into the restaurant, but from
time to time people would stop and peer in through my

window, shading their eyes with their hands. They wanted
to find out if the restaurant was open, and on finding that
it was they went on their way. Inside, nothing at all happened until five young people emerged from the big dining room at the back, coming through on their way to the
street. There were four boys and a girl, and they all seemed
to be about the same age — eighteen or nineteen. The girl
was very pretty, with straight blond hair, and the boys were
nice-looking. They were all dressed in blue jeans and
sweaters, and they looked quietly about them with a curiosity that was remarkable because it was polite and re-
served and at the same time perfectly alive and unashamed. Before they reached the door, the owner, Guy,
called to them in French and offered them a drink. *"Eau
sucrée,"* he said, and he laughed at them. They were at the
door, but they trooped over to the bar and sat up on the
high stools. They were all French, visiting here. They
talked with Guy and seemed to be just as interested in him
as they were in one another. I thought they looked incapa-
ble of rudeness or boredom. They were very happy, enjoying their idleness, and in their lack of self-consciousness I
saw the international elegance I had looked for at the
Waldorf. I did not listen closely enough to understand
what they were saying. I looked out into the street, not to
stare at them, and I thought their voices described them as
the pigeons in flight outside my hotel-room window describe the view that lies before me there. I am at the Beaux
Arts Hotel, on East Forty-fourth Street between First
Avenue and Second, and my room is on the twelfth floor,

with a great drop down to the flat roof of the adjoining house, so I have a clear view across low roofs and then across First Avenue to the glittering glass walls of the United Nations building and beyond to the East River and across the river to Queens. Just to the right of my window there is a monumentally ornate apartment building with four stone lions sitting upright on the corners of one of its lesser roofs. The lions wear crowns and hold iron pennants in their paws, but crowns, pennants, and paws are all subservient to the pigeons, who perch where they please and fly freely about the long, flowered terraces of the same building. Away over to the left, on the other side of Forty-fourth Street, there are low, moderately old commercial buildings, blank-faced, as well they might be, because they are surely doomed to come down soon, with all the ambitious construction work that is going on over there. On top of one of those buildings there is a big homemade terrace, hopefully painted pink. It is all the same to the pigeons. All of the buildings, high and low, are only different levels of the great arena in which they play all day, and they own everything in sight and out of sight. As I listened to the voices at the bar, I began to imagine I knew a country where people were so at ease with themselves that they were able to be at ease anywhere. I was thinking of another world, not France. Then, to my surprise, I saw the five young French people on the sidewalk outside my window, and as I watched they walked away down the street and out of my sight. They had made their adieus and left and I had heard nothing. Now they were gone and my lunch was finished, but I was not yet ready to leave. I watched the entrance to the back room until the waiter appeared, and I asked him for another *café-filtre*. I don't really like *café-filtre*, but when I am in French restaurants I always drink it. I think those dutiful *café-filtres* are probably all I will ever know of Marseille.

JULY 20, 1963

Sixth Avenue Shows Its True Self

L ATELY I have been taking oblong walks, staying between Fifty-ninth Street and Forty-fifth Street and keeping to four avenues — Sixth, Fifth, Madison, and Park. I am generally by myself, and I find that the separate personalities of these four avenues within this area have impressed themselves so insistently on me that I want to make a few remarks about them.

I have been searching for some good thing to say about Sixth Avenue, but I have failed in my search. Sixth Avenue shows its true self only during the two hours after dawn, when it is almost empty of life. During those hours, in the silence and the nice clean light, the eerie, unsubstantial disorderliness of those blocks of structures becomes apparent, and anyone walking alone through that ugliness can see without any trouble that Sixth is not a human thoroughfare at all but only a propped-up imitation of a thoroughfare, and that its purpose is not to provide safe or pleasant or beautiful passage for the people of the city but to propitiate, even if it is only for a little while, whatever the force is that feeds on the expectation of chaos. Those blocks, as far as you can see, offer nothing except the threat, or the promise, that they *will* come tumbling down. The buildings have about them nothing of the past and nothing of the future, no intimation of lives spent or to come, but only a reminder of *things* that should not have happened and a guarantee of *things* that should not come to pass.

Fifth Avenue is different. Fifth Avenue is fine and wide and satisfactory in every respect, but the shops all seem very far apart. They are not, of course — they are side by side, in the usual way — but walking takes longer and is more of an effort on Fifth than on the other avenues because the width of the sidewalks encourages a zigzag progress; instead of walking in or with or against the crowd, as I do on an ordinary sidewalk, I am encouraged by all the extra space to dodge around the crowd and in and out of it. Fifth Avenue is at its best after eight o'clock at night and until eight o'clock in the morning. On shopping nights it does not put on its deserted look until after ten, and on Sunday mornings it is quiet enough even after ten.

Park Avenue wears such an air of vast indifference to humanity that it is never interesting to walk on. Its face is closed, and the beautiful beds of flowers that are planted all along its center only hint that the view would be duller without them. Park Avenue looks friendly at Christmastime, when all those big trees are lighted up, but it is obviously an avenue to be splendidly lived on, and not to be looked at or walked on.

My favorite avenue, good at any hour of the day or night, and at any season, is Madison. Whenever I walk along Madison Avenue, I think of fine clothes and gaiety and of the possibility of having both at once. The avenue, which seems to get narrower and more interesting every year, has a frivolous, relaxed air. It is even romantic. The shop windows are so close to the ground, or seem so close to the ground, and so near, that no matter how fast you walk you cannot help seeing what is in them, and the shop windows on the second floor are often even more fascinating than the ones below, so that you have to bend your head back to try to guess exactly what it is up there that you know you want very badly — the color of it is so nice or the shape so mystifying. Heaven forbid that there should ever be a riot in the city, but if there is I will go straight over to Madison Avenue with my stone or brick and I will shut my eyes and just throw, because there is hardly a window along there that does not contain something I would like to have.

All this time I have been trying to think of one good thing to say about Sixth Avenue. Now I remember the walk I took there on the morning of the last big snow. I was living on West Fifty-eighth Street at the time, and I was out of my hotel just after dawn, and I walked all the way down to Forty-fifth Street and saw hardly a soul. The snow had fallen thickly and was still falling. There was no sign that the snow would ever stop falling, and as I looked about me, making my way along, I could see no reason for it ever to stop falling. I looked at the buildings closest to me, and then I looked as far up as their tops, which were hidden in a hazy confusion of sky and snow, and I looked along Sixth Avenue as far as the falling snow would allow, and wherever I looked, the buildings had shed their tacky, temporary air, and appeared theatrically lost and desolate, as though they were in a movie and would soon flicker away and disappear forever. Therefore, I have this to say for Sixth Avenue: It is a perfect place for snow, and snow should always be falling there, tons and tons and tons of snow, making the avenue just about impassable, so that anybody managing to struggle through there could look at it with affection, because Sixth Avenue possesses a quality that some people acquire, sometimes quite suddenly, which dooms it and them to be loved only at the moment when they are being looked at for the very last time.

NOVEMBER 4, 1961

I Look Down from the Windows of This Old Broadway Hotel

FROM the windows I have on the eleventh floor of this old Broadway hotel, I look down on West Forty-eighth Street, where the roofs of a few little houses that survive down there make a deep well inside the tall city that has grown up around them. Broadway is on my right — Broadway and all the big lights. A trombonist from the Latin Quarter appears on its roof every evening and gives a concert all by himself and to nobody. At that point the roof is only a story and a half high, and the crowd hurrying along just below him must be deafened by the Broadway din, because no one ever seems to stop to look up at him. Up here where I am, I can hear him very clearly. He comes up during intermission time, I suppose, and he saunters about for a minute, getting exercise, and then he walks to the edge of the roof and begins to play. He plays to the stars and he plays to the street and he plays for himself, with a large flourish to the right, a large flourish to the left. He is a heavyset man in a white shirt and black trousers, and his stage is a blackened roof that slants down to where he stands, with his toes almost touching the dazzling river of white and yellow neon light that rushes around the walls of the club. He stands in the middle of a vast explosion of restless light — every sign on Broadway going full blast — but he would be invisible if it were not for the whiteness of his shirt and the shine of his trombone. Those Broadway lights are selfish. They illuminate only themselves. The trombonist doesn't care. On his shelf of darkness, in the middle of all the splendor, he performs as devotedly as though he had the world at his feet.

One evening he turned up on the roof at seven, clearly visible in the azure autumn air. He took his stand at the roof's edge and began to play, and at that moment an extremely tall young man stood up between the two blue-painted water towers of the Flanders Hotel (twelve stories high, to my left) and began playing the clarinet. They both seemed to be playing "A Gypsy Told Me." The trombonist, a few stories above the crowded street, faced east, and the clarinetist, half a block away from him and twelve stories up in the air, also faced east, and all around them, above and below, on both sides, and in all directions, far and near and high and low, they were surrounded by walls of windows — hundreds and hundreds and hundreds of windows — and all the windows were blind, because there was not a face to be seen at any of them.

This is just about the center of the theatrical and entertainment section of New York City, but what joviality and good fellowship exist here are thin; the atmosphere is of shabby transience, and its heart is inimical. It is a run-down neighborhood of cheap hotels and rooming houses and offices and agencies and studios and restaurants and bars, and of shops that pack up and disappear overnight. If you walk along the street, you will find it busy, crowded, colorful, untidy, and with a fly-by-night air that makes it rakish, but in the first, unrested light of morning, which comes up very suddenly here, the irregular roof lines have a stoical despondency, and the blank windows reflect an extremity of loneliness — that mechanical city loneliness which strays always at the edge of chaos, far from solitude. The small houses down there mark the remains of a street where ordinary life used to be lived — ordinary social life, domestic life, real life, with children and parents and grandparents and uncles and family friends, with Christmas trees and schoolbooks and wedding dresses and birthdays — but it has come to be hardly more than a camping ground for strollers and travelers and tourists and transients of every kind. They all move on. A few people stay around here because they have no choice, and some stay because they are attached to the neighborhood for old times' sake and cannot bear to leave, although they can barely afford to stay. Each person is sealed off from the next person, sealed off even from the people he exchanges good mornings with, as though by fear of betrayal. An old woman living by herself in a single hotel bedroom goes frantic with apprehension and picks up the telephone, but there is no one for her to call. She tries to tell the room clerk of what is threatening her, and he listens, but he has the switchboard to attend to, and he has to watchdog the street entrance and the elevators, and he has other duties, and, in any case, he has heard her story many times before, from other people, in other years and in other defeated places like this one. The old woman puts the phone back and realizes immediately that she has made a bad mistake. It is a mistake she has guarded against until now. She knows perfectly well that she must not call attention to herself. This is her last stand in the land of the living, and she is here only on sufferance. The hotel won't miss her if she goes, and it can rent her room in a minute. She must not complain and she must watch her step. She must be more than polite; she must be obsequious. If you are old and poor and you get the hotel maid against you, you are out of luck.

This hotel was very grand when it was built, in 1902, but it has slid downhill. The lobby has been cut down to a fraction of what it was, and the ornate old ceiling, towering up there, makes a sad cavern of the small, mean space where the desk and the elevators are. The lobby used to be immense, with an orchestra playing and (I am told) a fountain, and along the back wall there was a row of noble windows that overlooked the gardens of the little Forty-eighth Street houses — the ones I can see from my windows. Three of the gardens are still there, but they are more or less rubbish now, and three others, together with their houses, have been erased to make a parking lot. The parking lot is busy all day and half the night, but at dawn it is deserted except by the pigeons, who fly down from the eaves and roofs and collect in a flock there to peck about peacefully, like barnyard fowl, while a thin mother cat, a stray, leads her family of kittens, who do not know yet that they are strays, in and out among the garbage cans that line the foot of this hotel and of the restaurants next door. But the morning wears on and the city begins to hustle. By half past eleven this morning, the pigeons and the cats had gone from the parking lot, and cars had parked there, and the restaurants up and down the street were busy getting ready for the lunchtime rush.

I have two very big rooms up here on the eleventh floor

— two big, shapely, spacious rooms, with folding doors between them. The ceilings are high, and the walls are so thick that I never hear a sound from inside the building. From outside I hear many sounds. I hear the cats and the pigeons and the cars, and I hear church bells, fire engines, garbage machines and the unearthly clatter of garbage cans, horses' hooves, radio music, singing, voices shouting, calling, laughing, denouncing, and screaming, glass breaking, airplanes, hammering, rain, the trombone-playing, and the roar of Broadway. Then today, at eleven-thirty, I heard some other music — the music of a very small band — and the tune being played was small and sweet and noticeably free: elfin music. The music came from Broadway, and I felt sorry for myself, because I thought that there must be a parade going on and that I would have only a glimpse of it as it passed the corner of Forty-eighth Street. But the music came closer, and then, at the western side of the parking lot, a man came slowly into view. He wore a dark blue suit and a military cap of the same blue. He was the band. The drum was strapped in front of him, and balanced on it was a plate for people to throw money into. The cymbal was fastened to his left side, and he clashed it with something fastened to the inside of his left arm. The trumpet, the drumstick, and all the small pieces of his equipment were attached to him by strings, and the reason he moved so slowly was that he had almost no legs. His legs had been cut off far above the knee, but he had enough power left in them to work his way along in what was not a walk but an adamant advance, and, all the time, he played. He looked very small. He banged the drum and blew the trumpet and clashed the cymbals and piped on a little pipe, but although the street was fairly busy, nobody gave him any attention that I could see, and nobody gave him any money. He appeared as indifferent to those around him as they were to him and his music, but as he moved along he kept turning his head to look into the parking lot. He was very much interested in the parking lot. He examined it. He looked it over. He seemed to be considering it. Maybe he was only doing what we often do when we are alone in public: hide our faces by pretending an interest in whatever presents itself — anything, as long as it cannot stare back. I do not know. Suddenly a car drove into the parking lot at such high speed that when it stopped, the brakes screamed horribly, but before it stopped, as it hurtled across the sidewalk, it came so close to the musician's back that I was sure it had brushed him. I got a fright, but the musician showed no sign of fright, or anxiety, or anger — not a sign of interest. He continued banging the drum, clashing the cymbal, blowing the trumpet; his music never faltered. Imperturbable, he advanced along his way and passed out of my sight behind the little houses just below me. His blithe, innocent music grew fainter and then faded, and I couldn't hear him anymore. I thought he might turn around and come back to Broadway this way, but he did not come back — at least, not while I waited.

OCTOBER 21, 1967

Mr. Sam Bidner and His Saxophone

NOT one man of the amiable company having dinner together at the Adano Restaurant on New Year's Eve held a lower rank than captain. There were Captain James Ancona, Captain Mickey Fields, Captain Joe Linder, Captain Bob Freed, and Captain Tom Shaw. Then there were Assistant Maître d' Eddie Femine, Maître d' Gigi, Night Manager Harry Spector, Banquet Manager Sonny Dall, Stage Manager Ernie D'Amato, Musical Director Sammy Fields (show music), Musical Director Sammy Bidner (dance music), Manager Henry Tobias, and Page Jack Hunter, who wore his page uniform, all buttons. These men constituted all the big brass of the Latin Quarter, and they were strengthening themselves at the Adano before going back to their own glittering palace to face the fiercest night of the year in the biggest night club in New York City. It was a snowy evening, not very cold — one of those nights when the Empire State Building smokes with light. And it was very early, not yet six o'clock. At that hour, the groups of people patrolling Broadway and the Broadway area nearly all included little children, who were being treated to their last glimpse of Christmas lights and Christmas trees before having their last dinner of the Old Year and going home to sleep the New Year in. At the Adano, the men from the Latin Quarter were eating their heads off. They started out with fish salad and went on to antipasto — stuffed mushrooms, roasted peppers, artichoke hearts in olive oil, pickled mushrooms, and more. Then they had green salad, linguine with lobster sauce, yards of Italian bread (both brown and white), cheesecake, and coffee. There were also two orders of linguine with white clam sauce, one order of spaghetti with meatballs, one order of veal scallopini with lemon sauce, a great many orders of lobster Fra Diavolo, and two orders of steak. The men all drank Italian wine. They were a handsome crowd, too alert-looking to be called worldly and too worldly-looking not to be called worldly. They sat together at a long table that had been arranged down the center of the room for them, and they all wore dark clothes — business suits or tuxedos — except Mr. Eddie Femine and Mr. Sammy Bidner. Mr. Femine, who is tall and debonair, wore a beige turtleneck, and Mr. Bidner wore a sporty-looking houndstooth-checked jacket with vents at the sides. Mr. Bidner had brought a small saxophone with him, and he played it every time he stood up from his place, halfway down the long table. He stood up very often. Some of his colleagues were late, and every time a new arrival walked in from the street, Mr. Bidner went forward to serenade him. Mr. Bidner walks very lightly and quickly, and he appears to move without making a sound, as though he remained always an inch or so above the ground and could make a complete turn, or two or three complete turns, without changing his posture or his expression and without losing a note of his music. I think he could move quickly backward for a long time without ever needing to look over his shoulder. He has beetling black eyebrows, and the expression of his eyes preserves the same high intensity whether he is looking at a stranger or talking with a friend or making a minute examination of some mysterious point in the near distance. He seems to look through what is present in the room but not beyond it. When he is not playing his saxophone, his expression is self-contained and at the same time conspiratorial. He appears to live at a high rate of speed, perhaps because he moves so softly. When he plays he crouches slightly, and when he is not playing he stands back ready to begin playing again. He is either playing or not playing, and his restless, attentive eyes give no sign of what he sees or of what he notices, and no sign of what he is thinking. His hairdo is Dickensian. Above his huge black eyebrows his bald pate shines round and unashamed, but he has a thick fringe of black hair around the sides and back of his head. Along the edges of the room, by the walls, ordinary Adano customers were sitting here and there having dinner, and Mr. Bidner went to each table and played a request tune. Anything he was asked for he played with all his might. There was a balloon master present. Mr. Ernie D'Amato can blow balloons into any shape he pleases: dogs, cats, giraffes — even automobiles, I suppose. Some of us at the Adano would have liked to see a balloon animal being made, but we had not brought any balloons with us, and Mr. D'Amato's tuxedo had just come back from the cleaners; his pockets

were empty — no balloons. He could only smile regretfully, a toymaker on holiday. That was a busy table. The
Adano waiters, who usually move about at an ordinary
pace, flew up and down the room so fast that they were
like shadows of themselves, and the dinner seemed to be
still going on when suddenly it was all over and the party
began to break up as the men started back to take up their
posts at the Latin Quarter. They went out in twos and
threes, all smiling and cheerful, no complaints. Everybody
had had a very good dinner. It was still snowing out, but
from the Adano to the Latin Quarter is a short distance
— along Forty-eighth Street and across Seventh Avenue
to where the big night club stands on its own small private
island between Seventh and Broadway. Assistant Maître d'
Eddie Femine stayed behind to check the bill. He stood at
the bar, reading carefully, while Joe Pariante, night manager of the Adano, watched him. Mr. Femine was very
quiet until he came to one item, which caused him to raise
his head and look disagreeably at Joe Pariante. *"Two dollars a portion! Who do you think you are?"* he yelled, and
then, laughing like a television maniac, he went back to his
careful checking. It was Mr. Femine's little joke. He was
pretending to be an ordinary customer. Behind the bar,
Bob, who looks imperturbable whether he is smiling or
serious, smiled. When the bill was paid, Eddie Femine
congratulated Joe Pariante on the food, the wine, the service, and the atmosphere, and wished him a Happy New
Year, and left. He was the last of the Latin Quarter crowd

to go, and when Josephine, the hat-check lady, had seen him out she sat down in the end booth and beamed. "Weren't they nice?" she said. "Weren't they nice?" Every Adano customer gets two warm welcomes from Josephine — one welcome on arrival, one on departure. For New Year's Eve she wore a black-and-silver tunic dress and her hair was newly rinsed with Miss Clairol's Moongold. With all the Latin Quarter crowd gone, the Adano seemed very quiet. Joe Pariante leaned against the bar and allowed himself to look wild-eyed for a minute, but the telephone rang and he had to answer it. He came back to say, "A party from Radio City Music Hall wants a table for ten at nine-thirty. That was Freddie Pasqualone calling." His was the last reservation accepted. The Adano was booked up until midnight. It was going to be a big evening, but not yet. The clock said a quarter to seven. There was plenty of time. The waiters began walking around at their ordinary speed, and soon the tables that had been put together for the big party were separated and dressed up with fresh linen and glasses and silver. The Adano stopped looking as though New Year's Eve were over and began looking like itself again. Joe Pariante remembered that some of the fish salad was left, and that he wanted to show it around. Fish salad is not on the menu at the Adano. It was specially ordered by the Latin Quarter ahead of time. Shrimp, *scungilli, calamari,* and octopus, cut up into small pieces, with lemon, oil, garlic, and red-seeded hot pepper — that is fish salad, and it looks delicious. When it had been admired and exclaimed over, Joe took the dish to the window refrigerator, where people going by on the street can see bottles of wine, a basket of pears and apples and grapes, and antipasto, red and green.

It was still snowing out. Forty-eighth Street in that block is a musicians' street, with a great many shops selling musical instruments and sheet music, and then there are practice studios and teachers' studios. Diagonally across from the Adano, the second-floor window of Frank Wolf Drummers' Supplies was dimly lighted to show glittering tinsel scattered across a row of drums of different colors and sizes — there were a royal blue drum, a pale blue drum, a turquoise drum, and a pink drum, and two gold drums, one bright and shining and one in dull gold. Through the snow and the darkness, the little window of drums and tinsel looked like a still life of New Year's Eve. It would be nice to think that all those men from the Latin Quarter would come back to the Adano next New Year's Eve and have exactly the same dinner and make the same jokes, and that Mr. Sammy Bidner would play his saxophone around the room again. But next New Year's Eve there won't be a Forty-eighth Street. A number of houses are already down, and on weekdays the street is filled with that choking white wreckers' dust. Forty-eighth Street is going, going. Office Space must be served, but somebody should write a Lament for Forty-eighth Street — a cheerful lament, because Forty-eighth has always been a cheerful street. And who, by the way, is Freddie Pasqualone?

Freddie Pasqualone is a member of the Radio City Music Hall Symphony Orchestra. He plays the trumpet.

JANUARY 20, 1968

The Ailanthus, Our Back-Yard Tree

THE ailanthus, New York City's back-yard tree, has been appearing around Broadway lately. "Appearing" is the exact word, because the ailanthus appears, like a ghost, like a shade, beyond the vacancy left by the old brownstone houses that are coming down one two three four five these days. From the north and from the south and from the east, Office Space is advancing on Broadway, and the small side streets west of Sixth Avenue are going fast. Behind the old houses, only shreds remain of the original back yards or gardens, but when the houses come down the ailanthus appears — the tenacious ailanthus, growing up, well nourished, in its scrap of earth. The first of the Broadway ailanthuses I saw appeared on Forty-ninth Street, beyond the empty hole left by the brownstone where the gypsies used to be. The gypsies had had the first floor of the house, and they had taken over the front steps as well. The old house hadn't been changed much, and nine worn steps with iron treads led up to the entrance. Somebody had made the ascent narrower and easier with low iron railings, and on summer nights the gypsies congregated there, and the young women among them stood and leaned against the railings while the small gypsy children swung and tumbled about on the railings. When I looked across the street one day, after the wreckers had been at work on that block for quite a while, and saw the ailanthus — two ailanthuses, in fact — I was startled, and I stood and looked at them, and said to them, "Were you there all the time?" That first day the two ailanthus trees were green under a blue November sky. It was sixty-five degrees that afternoon, unseasonable weather, but the ailanthuses accepted the warm sunshine serenely, and made shadows of themselves against the high, blank wall beyond them. The Forty-ninth Street ailanthus trees are skeletons now — thin skeletons, meticulously defined by the blank wall that juts out from the back of one of the Sixth Avenue buildings. The trees will soon be gone, and so will the blank wall, because that area between Forty-ninth and Fiftieth is being flattened to make way for the latest Rockefeller office building, a fifty-four-story skyscraper that will probably be the new Esso Building, according to the *Times*. On these Broadway side streets, where the architecture is so mixed and often so unfortunate, the brownstones, the handsomest houses of them all, come down the most quickly. One minute the brownstone is standing, deserted, stripped, and empty, and the next minute its roof is gone and its front is gone and its insides are showing, daylight streaming like cold water over curved staircases and papered walls and small inte-

riors — doors and ceilings and corners that remain secret
even with everybody looking at them. Then, when it is all
over and the house is gone and the thick white dust has
settled, there is the ailanthus, speaking of survival and of
ordinary things. These days in New York, when Order and
Chaos shadow each other so closely that it is hard to tell
the difference between them, the ailanthus stands up like a
sign of reality. The new Office Space giants have nothing
to do with our daily lives, or with ordinary things, and
they are taking away our streets.

The side streets off Broadway have always been
crammed with small enterprises of every description, and
with small restaurants. There used to be hundreds of restaurants, of every nationality and of varying degrees of
charm and atmosphere and price. What all those restaurants had in common was that each place was owned by
the man who stood behind the bar, or by the man who
stood behind the cash register, or by the man who came
forward to meet you when you walked in. We ordinary
New Yorkers were kings and lords in all those places, even
where the owner pretended to be surly, even where he
really was surly. We could pick and choose and find our
favorites, and so enjoy one of the normal ways of making
ourselves at home in the city. It is in daily life, looking
around for restaurants and shops and for a place to live,
that we find our way about the city. And it is necessary to
find one's own way in New York. New York City is not
hospitable. She is very big and she has no heart. She is not

charming. She is not sympathetic. She is rushed and noisy and unkempt, a hard, ambitious, irresolute place, not very lively, and never gay. When she glitters she is very, very bright, and when she does not glitter she is dirty. New York does nothing for those of us who are inclined to love her except implant in our hearts a homesickness that baffles us until we go away from her, and then we realize why we are restless. At home or away, we are homesick for New York not because New York used to be better and not because she used to be worse but because the city holds us and we don't know why.

Manhattan is an island, and so she has two horizons — the architectural horizon, impermanent and stony, and the eternal horizon, constantly changing, that is created when water and sky work together in midair. It may be that the secret of Manhattan's hold over us is lost somewhere between those two horizons, the one hard and vulnerable, the other vague, shifting, and implacable. All we can be sure of is that she has a secret that binds us to her — something unresting and restless, something she shares with us even though we are not allowed to understand it. Other cities are mysterious. Amsterdam and London and Hong Kong are mysterious. Rome and Berlin are mysterious. New York is not mysterious. New York is a mystery. What is this place where Chaos stretches and sits down and makes himself at home? We live here, and we become part of the mystery. With Chaos, we make ourselves at home. We find our way about and establish a daily life for

ourselves. But more and more the architecture of this city
has nothing to do with our daily lives. The Office Space
giants that are going up all over Manhattan are blind
above the ground, and on the ground level they are given
over to banks and to showrooms, and to businesses run by
remote control by companies and corporations rich
enough to afford the staggering rents. The smooth, narrow thoroughfares created by the office skyscrapers are
deadly to walk through in the daytime, and at night they
are silent and dangerous. The newly depressed areas of our
city are very rich.

At this moment I am sitting at a table in the English
Grill and I am looking out into Rockefeller Plaza. The
Promenade Café is bright and cheerful, with the vaguely
institutional air common to restaurants run by remote
control — restaurants where the host is not the owner. It
is a benign institutionalism, not bad at all once you get
used to it. Sitting here by the big glass wall, I am a part of
the crowd outside in the plaza. The plaza is spectacular,
with its stone terraces and stone steps, and with the long
and lingering vistas of stone and light and shadow that
occur between and through the surrounding towers of
Rockefeller Center. In the skating rink the skaters go
round and round. I wonder if the ailanthus will ever appear in Rockefeller Plaza. I suppose not. The ailanthus is a
back-yard tree, and Rockefeller Plaza is a private back
yard only one day each year. Every July, for the length of
one Sunday, the plaza is closed to the public. On all the

other days, members of the public are allowed to come and go in the plaza, free of charge. And the ailanthus is wild. It grows like a weed. There are no weeds in Rockefeller Plaza. The plaza is monumentally correct in every detail, and its key monument, the massive John D. Rockefeller, Jr., memorial stone, has not a scratch on it, not even a smudge. The memorial stone is a huge, severely cut wedge of polished dark green marble, and it is set into the top of the steps at the eastern end of the skating rink. The side of the stone facing the rink bears a bas-relief in bronze of Mr. Rockefeller's head and, underneath:

JOHN D. ROCKEFELLER, JR.
1874–1960
FOUNDER OF ROCKEFELLER CENTER

The reverse side of the stone, facing the flowered promenade that leads to Fifth Avenue, is slanted for easy reading, and is deeply engraved with the ten points of Mr. Rockefeller's personal credo, his "I Believe." To anyone approaching the stone from Fifth Avenue, the engraved words stare out with the dark and awful command of a prophecy. Here are Mr. Rockefeller's words:

I BELIEVE
I believe in the supreme worth of the individual and in his right to life, liberty, and the pursuit of happiness.
I believe that every right implies a responsibility; every opportunity, an obligation; every possession, a duty.

I believe that the law was made for man and not man for the law; that government is the servant of the people and not their master.

I believe in the dignity of labor, whether with head or hand; that the world owes no man a living but that it owes every man an opportunity to make a living.

I believe that thrift is essential to well ordered living and that economy is a prime requisite of a sound financial structure, whether in government, business or personal affairs.

I believe that truth and justice are fundamental to an enduring social order.

I believe in the sacredness of a promise, that a man's word should be as good as his bond; that character — not wealth or power or position — is of supreme worth.

I believe that the rendering of useful service is the common duty of mankind and that only in the purifying fire of sacrifice is the dross of selfishness consumed and the greatness of the human soul set free.

I believe in an all-wise and all-loving God, named by whatever name, and that the individual's highest fulfillment, greatest happiness, and widest usefulness are to be found in living in harmony with His will.

I believe that love is the greatest thing in the world; that it alone can overcome hate; that right can and will triumph over might.

— JOHN D. ROCKEFELLER, JR.

Architecturally, very little that was notable has been lost in the destruction of the Broadway area. What has been lost is another strip of the common ground we share with each other and with our city — the common ground that is all that separates us from the Machine. Mr. Rockefeller's words stand up to be read by everyone who walks through Rockefeller Plaza. Perhaps the architects of the proposed Esso Building will consider memorializing the words of another New Yorker, a man whose only house was made of wood and built on sand. How enjoyable to see engraved, *in marble,* on a wall of the new Rockefeller skyscraper: "Where it all will end, knows God! — Wolcott Gibbs."

MARCH 23, 1968

A Little Boy Crying

I SAW a little boy on the street today, and he cried so eloquently that I will never forget him. He was going down the subway steps into the station at Seventy-seventh Street and Lexington Avenue. There is a big flower shop on the corner there, and its window overlooks the steps. The window was filled high with spring flowers today, a calm and silent conflagration behind the glass, and across the middle of the glass, like skywriting, a single line of red neon spelled out DANA'S FLOWER SHOP. On this gray day the flowers in the window glowed, but the red of the neon sign was both raw and suffused — the color of pressure, if we could see pressure. The little boy who cried was six or seven years old, and he was bundled up too tightly in heavy clothes. He wore his dark winter clothes, although we were having one of those damp, irresolute days that turn with the wind from mild to chilly. The boy was carrying a schoolbag, a kind of fat briefcase, and it banged against his legs as he came along Lexington toward the subway entrance — partly through his own fault, because he was running from side to side behind his mother, peering up at her, trying to find which side gave him a better view of her face. He wanted to be sure she heard his scolding. His voice went on and on. He had an enormous amount of energy in his voice — hard energy. She was carrying two shopping bags and a large handbag and a large, square parcel, which she held high against her chest. The parcel forced her chin up. The child hadn't a chance of seeing her face, and, in any case, her expression said that all she was thinking of was when she would get a chance to sit down. She was young and fat and walking very fast, with her black raincoat swinging open. The little boy and his schoolbag tumbled around behind her as though they were attached to the back of her coat collar by elastic string. There was another child, a boy of about nine, who strode beside the mother in independence, carrying a bigger schoolbag in one hand and a loaded shopping bag in the other. I first saw the three of them as they approached Dana's doorway, which is only a step from the subway entrance. As they passed the doorway, the little boy stopped harrying his mother and began harrying his brother, who glanced absently at him, as if he were a chair, and got him out of the way with a good push of the big schoolbag. The little boy stopped scolding and ran back to his mother to demand justice. She had turned the corner by the flower shop, and, very carefully, she started down the steps. She was concentrating on keeping her balance, and her attention was farther than ever from her younger son. The older boy had slipped ahead of his mother and run down the steps, and he was waiting at the bottom, not looking up but looking away into the station. The smaller boy, following his mother, put his right hand up to the handrail to steady himself, and so had to change his schoolbag from his right hand to his left. When he realized that both his hands were now held, one by the rail and the other by the schoolbag, he stood still on the step and gathered his strength and began to denounce his mother while continuing to try to explain to her that his brother had pushed him. But the anger that had been churning around inside him while he was in motion must have gained in power when he stopped moving, because all his words turned into gasps that imprisoned him so that he could cry only two sounds — or, rather, two notes on one sound. The sound was "Aaaaaaaah!" and the notes were of denunciation and reproach. Denunciation was the hard note and reproach was the pitiful minor note. While he continued to cry with all his strength, his face turned a solid pale red that was closer in color and feeling to Dana's neon sign than it was to any of the flowers in the window. The two notes continued like a lament. It was a lament.

The little boy was singing on two notes. There was no end to his grief. He was completely betrayed, his song said, and it continued even after he began to climb slowly down the steps to his mother, who was calling desperately to him from below. His lament went on and on, growing fainter but remaining unmistakable as he descended. He might have been the last bird in the world, except that if he had been the last bird there would have been no one to hear him.

APRIL 27, 1968

A Young Man with a Menu

LATE this afternoon, in the Longchamps at Twelfth Street and Fifth Avenue, I watched a young man persuade a girl to join him for dinner by reading the menu to her over the telephone. He stood in the glass telephone booth by the huge street window and read here and there from the menu, suggesting things to eat, and from time to time he fell silent and listened to whatever the voice at the other end of the phone was saying. The voice seemed to have a good deal more to say than he had, and each time, after he had listened to it for a while, he stopped staring and lifted the menu in front of himself as though it were a hook that would drag her back to the point he wanted to make. He wanted her to have dinner with him. There was snow falling outside — a steady fluttering of modest little flakes that turned into gray fluff as soon as they touched the sidewalk. Every once in a while, a fierce gale tore down the avenue from the north, sending the snowflakes streaming away toward Washington Square, and then the whole view seemed to blow up, and looked white and dangerous. It was getting dark. Across the street, the heavy stone of the massive building where the Macmillan Company used to be made a somber background for the pandemonium, and the bookshop next door, Dauber & Pine, had all its lights on but still managed to suggest a shadowy and mysterious interior, making it the very picture of an old bookshop seen through the dusk of a wintry day — a wintry day in spring, as it is now. The great sheet of glass that allows this theatrical view of Fifth Avenue is really a movable wall that rolls back in the good weather to open the restaurant to the sidewalk café. It is an arrangement that turns the whole Fifth Avenue front of the restaurant into a stage set.

Tonight, shut in from all the wildness and clamor outside, Longchamps was very quiet and warm, and almost deserted. The young man who read the menu over the phone had not yet made his appearance when I arrived. There was hardly anyone at the long, long bar, which looked lonely; only a few people were having drinks or dinner; there were mostly empty tables in the big, comfortable room; and the back room, which is even bigger, was just as quiet. Some years ago they lowered the ceilings in this branch of Longchamps and made a great many other alterations that banished every trace of the awkward, cavernous, romantic atmosphere the place used to have, but the front room is saved from being completely conventional by the arrangement of the sidewalk café. The café is carpeted in green and has a low marbled wall of faded pink coral with a miniature hedge of green box along the top of it, so that in summer people sitting out there are half hidden from the passersby, and all year round all we in the restaurant can see of the passersby is what shows of them above the hedge — the upper parts of their bodies, their shoulders and heads. The café awning, printed on the inside with pink apple blossoms, extends down to within a couple of feet of the top of the little hedge, so that the view of the Avenue, wild and snowy tonight, is sliced off at the top by apple blossoms and from below by the spiky green box, making the setting even more theatrical. Tonight, with darkness coming on and everything tossing about out there, it seemed as though that scrap of Fifth Avenue had been set up as the starting point of a very interesting movie. Any minute now, the star of the movie would come into view, walking past the hedge with the rest of the people who were struggling along out there, but he would turn away from the crowd and walk through the opening in the hedge and push his way through the revolving door. We would get only glimpses of him across the top of the hedge and then see him vaguely through the glass panels of the door, but after that he would step into the restaurant and look decisively about him, registering his personality, before he walked straight to the bar, or straight to a certain table. He would

be wearing a raincoat. It would be a spy movie, with perhaps a murder and certainly a chase. All these empty
tables would make good hurdling, and there were just
about enough customers to register fear, horror, glee, and
so on. And all the waiters and waitresses were at their
stations, in full fig. Full fig for the waitresses at this Longchamps means a blue-and-gray-striped dress — a very
unfair garb, unbecoming to the girls and depressing for
the customers, but one that might lend itself to all kinds of
sinister effects in the eye of an imaginative cameraman,
though it takes only a little imagination to connect those
stripes with crime and punishment. Almost any restaurant
provides a good opening scene for a movie about spies, but
the Longchamps at Twelfth and Fifth is ready-made for
episodes of intrigue and pursuit, because, in spite of all the
remodeling that has been done there, the back of the
restaurant — the far end of the back room — still seems
to stretch off into infinity. And across the avenue there is
the haunted-looking bookshop, the dour gray front of the
publishers' building, and the old Presbyterian church, with
its gardens and its railings. The noseless architecture we
are all growing accustomed to has dulled our view and will
soon cure us of our habit of gazing at the city we live in,
but this part of lower Fifth Avenue still allows us to dream
that there is room for life to go here and there in human
ways, off the mechanical paths.

The little hedge out there had gathered quite a lot of
snow when the young man who was to spend so much
time in the glass phone booth came into view, exactly as

the star of that movie might have made his entrance, head
and shoulders first across the hedge, and then full length
but blurred through the glass panels of the revolving door,
and then he was inside — still standing up, which was
lucky, because he was one of those who fumble and paw at
revolving doors instead of pressing themselves firmly
against them. He wore a big, crumpled raincoat, which
hung open so that the tartan lining showed. He was tubby
and not very tall, and he had straight, fine, sandy hair that
was plentiful except on top of his head, where it was very
thin — nearly all gone, in fact. He was about twenty-five,
or perhaps twenty-seven, with blue eyes and neat features
— a straight, tiny nose and a serious mouth. His expression as he entered the restaurant said that he was intent on
something — one thing — and indifferent to everything
else. He couldn't have walked very far; there was very little
snow on him. Under his arm he clutched a bundle of
London *Observer*s, which had been opened and folded
back carelessly so they looked half inflated and as though
they might start to rise, like a soufflé, at any minute. He
didn't look about him, or hesitate, but spoke anxiously to
the first face he saw, which belonged to the coatroom girl,
who was watching him across the half door of her little
cubicle, where she had a background of empty wall tonight — no customers, no coats. The girl answered him by
nodding toward the glass phone booth, and he went
quickly over and got into it and shut the door. He had his
dime ready, and he dialed at once and started talking,
holding the phone with the same air of anxiety he had

shown when he spoke to the coatroom girl. He never smiled. Even later, when he had won his suit on the telephone, he did not smile. He was serious in all his ways, and methodical — not as though he were naturally methodical but as though he had made up his mind that tonight he was going to make no false move. The occasion was so important to him that he was not himself. He was buried in the importance of that phone call. He spoke on the phone for a minute, and then he opened the door and stepped out of the booth, and when he stepped back in he had the big Longchamps menu in his left hand, and he took the phone in his right hand. The restless *Observers* were pinned down by his right elbow. And he had coins to manage and maneuver. He used up three more before the conversation ended. The young man was taking no chances, and he wasn't going to tempt the Fates by letting go of any of his encumbrances — he would hold on to all of them, like a man standing up in the subway at rush hour. He read from all sections of the menu. I had a menu of my own, so I could tell just about where he was — in Seafood, and in Desserts, and in Curries and Specialties, and in Salads, and so on. He read straight down the Sizzling Platters column, and something there may have decided her, and shut her up, because it all ended very suddenly. He hung up the phone and got himself out and went to the bar, which is on the north side of the room and looks about a mile long — more than a mile tonight, in its deserted state.

The young man put his *Observers* on one of the stools

near the window end, and then he turned and politely laid his menu on the nearest unoccupied table, and took off his raincoat and made it into a bundle to anchor the newspapers. And at last he stood still and looked around him, tightening the knot of his tie, which was much too tight and small already. Once he had taken the raincoat off, you could see that he was not tubby but sloppy. His navy blue suit was loose and almost as crumpled as his raincoat, and he wore a white shirt with a button-down collar, which went up quite far on his neck. The tie let itself go under the tiny knot and flowed in bright stripes of red and orange down to below the waistband of his trousers. His expression as he surveyed the restaurant was calm, and when he sat down he turned the stool sidewise to the bar and went on gazing benignly at the room. Most people sitting alone at that bar turn sidewise, because there is nothing facing them across the bar but a blank wall with, at its center, a towering cupboard of evangelical extraction that looks as though it might be musical. The young man put his hands on his thighs and sat there resting. He was not relaxing. What he was doing was much more old-fashioned — he was simply resting. The bartender brought him a bottle of beer and a tall glass, and after the young man had tasted the beer he picked up a little bowl of peanuts that was there on the bar and emptied some of the peanuts into his right hand. Then he went on resting, taking peanuts from his right hand with his left hand and looking around the restaurant.

It was time for me to leave, and as I collected my umbrella from the coatroom girl, somebody came through the revolving door, and I turned to look. She wore a red coat with a red hood attached, and she didn't throw the hood back, so I didn't see even the color of her hair. The young man had stood up and was looking at her, and his face wore the same expression it had had when he came in — he looked intent on something and indifferent to everything else. I went out. The sidewalk was positively dangerous, sliding away from me and everybody else, and the tall new apartment buildings that dwarf the Washington Arch seemed to shiver in their glittering skins. Those buildings give off a magnificent slaty light on wet nights. It is their only moment of beauty. The wind had turned bitter, perhaps because the snow had stopped falling, and it took me nearly fifteen minutes longer to walk home than it usually does.

APRIL 22, 1967

Painful Choice

I WAS in a new small supermarket the other evening, waiting to have my things put in a bag, when I saw a shabby tall man with red eyes, who had obviously been drinking heavily since the cradle, trying to decide between a can of beans, a canned whole dinner, a canned soup, and a canned chicken à la king. He had thirty-seven cents or twenty-nine cents or some sum like that, and he was standing there with the four cans, glaring down at them and all around at the stalls of vegetables and fruit and bread and so on. He couldn't make up his mind what to buy to feed himself with, and it was plain that what he really wanted wasn't food at all. I was thinking I wouldn't blame him a bit if he just put the cans back on their shelves, or dropped them on the floor, and dashed into the bar-and-grill next door, where he could simply ask for a beer and drink it. Later on it occurred to me that, putting it roughly, there is usually only one thing we yearn to do that's bad for us, while if we try to make the effort to do a virtuous or good thing, the choice is so great and wide that we're really worn out before we can settle on what to do. I mean to say that the impulse toward good involves choice, and is complicated, and the impulse toward bad is hideously simple and easy, and I feel sorry for that poor tall red-eyed man.

SEPTEMBER 18, 1954

The New Girls on West Forty-ninth Street

I HEARD bad news tonight at Le Steak de Paris, where I had dinner. "The building is coming down" — and the little restaurant is to be swept away, just like that, after more than twenty-six years of hardy life. Those words

"The building is coming down" occur so often in New York conversation, and they have such finality, and are so unanswerable, that once they have been said there is nothing more to say. There is no appealing the decisions of the ogre called Office Space that stalks the city and will not be appeased. Le Steak de Paris occupies the ground floor and the cellar of an old brownstone on West Forty-ninth Street, between Sixth Avenue and Seventh Avenue. Demolition has begun, but there are still several of the brownstones in a row — tall, thin nineteenth-century houses that stand as straight and plain as ever they did but seem to slant backward together because they are so out of line with the rest of the street. It is a broken-down, mismatched, patched-up street, and for many years it has existed in the extraordinary vacuum created by the city planners, who cast whole areas into limbo for long periods — for decades, sometimes — before the demolition workers actually move in. At the moment the dark shadow in New York is cast not by the past but by the future, and too many streets wear a dull air of "What's the use?" This particular block of West Forty-ninth Street is dingy and finished-looking in the daytime, but at night it is merely shabby, and when the lights are on in the restaurants and bars and around the hotel entrances it becomes garish and secretive — more like the extension of a carnival than like a city street. Broadway, the street of dreams, has about as much connection with the ordinary life of the city as a traveling circus would have, but although the area's image is steadily being transformed into a grimmer and more orderly one — the office-space image — the glamour of Broadway persists and spills over into the narrow side streets that lead to the big lights. All is makeshift on Forty-ninth Street, and even the old brownstones, so beautifully proportioned and presenting such a pure outline against the high, calm evening sky of summer, seem part of a stage set designed to illustrate the shaky and vanishing side of New York City. This is a tourist block, and they were nearly all tourists on the sidewalks tonight — out-of-towners in light-colored cottony dresses and suits, with jackets and sweaters over their arms. Diligent sightseers, they had been going around town all day, looking at the "points of interest," and now they plodded on toward their share of night life. Though the groups walking along were of all kinds, they were mostly couples, or parties of men and women walking together, or small parties of middle-aged women walking very close together. They formed little crowds along the street, peering through restaurant doorways and windows, wanting to see inside without quite wanting to go in. The pavement in front of Le Steak de Paris had just been swept clean, and the miniature box hedge at the window looked very fresh and green after last night's rain. No one was peering through the windows of Le Steak — it is too quiet there for visitors in search of excitement or novelty. There were a few people having dinner — very few — and two men, two solitaries, were drinking peacefully at the bar. I asked

the owner, M. Guy L'Heureux, whether he had found a
new home for his restaurant, and he sadly said, "No, not in
the city. It was very difficult. We were looking all the time,
everywhere. There was nothing. We have decided to move
to Miller Place, Long Island. We will learn English now.
There will be no one to speak French to." Inside, Le Steak
has hardly changed in all the years I have been going
there. The walls were once covered with printed-paper
murals of rustic eighteenth-century scenes. Later there
was red-brick-patterned wallpaper. Now the paper imi-
tates polished wooden planks — vertical planks — and
there is a cigarette machine where the jukebox that played
French records used to be. But nothing has really changed
there. The menu is much the same as always — Crème
Jeannette, Poulet Rôti, Shrimps Cocktail, Artichaut Froid,
and so on. Even the atmosphere is the same, as though
finality had stayed where it belongs — out of sight and far
away. M. Guy and Jo, the waiter, and Francine, the waitress, were all calm and cheerful, as though they expected to
be welcoming customers to Le Steak de Paris for a long
time to come. There are restaurants in the other brownstones, but the tenants who used to live upstairs in the old
houses have all moved away except one top-floor lady, who
clings to her apartment, where she has lived for years, and
still carefully tends potted plants on her windowsills. The
plants make a fragile show of green, a living frieze against
the old walls. When I left Le Steak, about nine-thirty, I
walked toward Seventh Avenue, which becomes Broad-

way at almost exactly the point where it meets Forty-ninth Street. I moved along slowly, with the slow, hesitating crowd. With all the hesitation, and all the slowness, there was no revelry. There never is, on West Forty-ninth Street. It is a tentative, transient, noisy street, very ill at ease and, to a stranger's eye, shifty, as though gaiety were unknown or strictly forbidden. Traffic is westbound in that block, so we all went along together, cars and people moving toward Broadway in a solid mass, almost as though we were on a pilgrimage. We passed the bouncy discothèque place next to Le Steak, and we passed Chinese restaurants and a Japanese restaurant and the record shop and the delicatessen and the hairdressing salon that stays open far into the night, and the Plymouth Hotel Coffee Shop, which never closes, and at last we reached the big parking garage. There's a pizza-hero place next to the entrance, and next to that, in what was once the doorway to the upper floors of the garage building, a gypsy has her parlor, a tiny place. Four stone steps lead up to her private door, which stood open tonight, though the gypsy was not to be seen. She had retreated to a back room, perhaps. But a vase of artificial flowers stood invitingly on a round table, and there was a small piece of carpeting on the tile floor. Next to the gypsy's parlor is an adults-only movie house that advertises itself with a frenzied blast of lights and signs. Tonight, the shows were *The Promiscuous Sex* and *Strip Poker Queens Wild.* The theater marquee is so dazzling that the letters of the titles always seem to jump into the air, blinding people half a block away, and it is surprising, when you finally reach the theater, to find a fairly clear space on the sidewalk in front of it, because hardly anybody lingers there. Tonight, at the edge of the clear space, to the side of the theater and at the foot of the gypsy's steps, five big young girls were standing around — not together, not in a group, but just standing around. The crowd was so thick up to that point that I didn't see the girls until I reached them. Nobody around me saw them, either, and although we were moving along and they were standing still, before we knew it they were upon us. It was like that, as though they had pounced, just as the lights seem to pounce, causing shame, or distress, or embarrassment, or curiosity, or derision, or excitement, or disgust, according to the nature of the person who sees them. This was one of those times of surprise when we cannot tell the difference between memory and instinct, between reminders and threats, and all was confusion, except that it was obviously important to avoid the eyes of those girls, because they were the eyes of satisfied furies, or of unsatisfied prison wardresses. The five never moved. They stood still, and the crowd broke up and detoured unsteadily around them. They were quite tall and about twenty years of age each, with straight, heavy hair dyed different shades of bronze and yellow and platinum, and they all wore tiny, frothy demi-mini shifts, which barely covered their behinds and seemed designed to show even more leg than they had. They were not slender girls. They looked

well fed, and their legs were solid and strong and female,
like pillars of flesh. One pair of legs was bare, a powdery-
pink color. The four other pairs were encased in neon-col-
ored fishnet stockings — two pairs in neon green, one pair
in neon mauve, and one pair in neon white that shone
with a pearly luster. The girls were probably not unusually
tall, but their legs made them look colossal. They were a
powerful group of young women, and people hurried past
them, glancing at them with the furtive attention most of
us give to the solemnly erotic photographs in the big
glass-covered case that stands outside the movie house. In
front of me there was a diminutive old lady with thickly
crimped hair dyed to a rich dark red, who kept turning to
stare back at the girls. She wore an imitation-leopard pillbox hat, and she was grinning, almost laughing. She spoke
to a woman walking next to her. "Did you see those
bums?" she said to the woman. The woman sprang away
from her without answering her, and the old lady turned
back and saw me. "Did you see those bums?" she said
delightedly to me. "Did you *see* those *bums*?" She looked
about ninety years old. It was my turn to hurry on ahead,
in order to get away from her, and I almost caught up with
the first woman to be addressed, who had joined two other
women, as quietly dressed, in suits and hats and gloves, as
she was herself. The three women reached the corner and
disappeared up Seventh Avenue, going as fast as they
could — home to their hotel, I think. I had a short wait on
the corner for a taxi. I didn't like to turn around for an-

other look at Forty-ninth Street, for fear of finding the imitation-leopard pillbox bobbing about behind me. But there was no need to fear any further word from her to me. When I did turn around, she had gone back along the street to where the girls were. I had a glimpse of her pillbox, and I am sure she was asking her question of other surprised people. A taxi came along, and I got into it and started home. Three or four summers ago, at about six o'clock in the evening, I saw a girl walking alone along Forty-ninth Street. She wore a red dress, and her walk was a ladylike travesty of Marilyn Monroe's walk, and she was swinging her handbag. All heads turned to stare at her as she sauntered boldly along in broad daylight, and she seemed very daring, but any one of the girls I saw tonight would make short work of her. Those girls looked as though they had been assembled, legs and all, in an automobile factory. They made Forty-ninth Street look very old-fashioned — faded, in fact, and harmless. They didn't go with the street at all. They were ahead of themselves by a year or two. They will go better with the new buildings.

SEPTEMBER 16, 1967

The View Chez Paul

TODAY, Saturday, was warm, windy, and gray, and for the first time this year the city showed its summer emptiness. The endless avenues were quiet and

looked wider, and people were scarce on the side streets. In
the middle of town, New York took on its desultory tourist
look, except in the block of Forty-fourth Street between
Fifth and Sixth, where there was pandemonium of the
locked, almost silent kind we who live in the city have
come to associate with the arrival of the moviemakers.
During the past few months, I have watched preparations
for moviemaking in several parts of town, and in every
case there was the same enormously organized cessation
of activity; it is as though invaders from another country
had arrived with all their trucks and their armies and their
heavy artillery, and with their battle plans drawn up, only
to find they had forgotten their ammunition, or their general. They wait. First they maneuver themselves and their
heavy equipment into position, and then they begin waiting. They drink coffee out of cardboard containers. They
speak together, but not very much. They have no need of
language. They annex what they want — this doorway,
that second-floor window, a corner of the park, a certain
stretch of street — and they ignore the rest, including us
New Yorkers, who stand about smiling and goggling like
friendly natives. The moviemakers hate to be asked questions. They hardly seem to see us. They are aloof, touched
by the remoteness of the Star that will begin shining now
at any minute. They wait. And, on the outside, we wait —
adults, children, and dogs, all of us crowding as close as we
can get to where the Presence will stand, the Star. The Star
on West Forty-fourth Street today was Julie Andrews. She
was making a movie in the Algonquin Hotel, and early

this afternoon the narrow street outside the hotel was
packed tight with her caravan. A caravan, according to my
dictionary, is a company traveling together for safety in the
East. Miss Andrews's caravan was extensive — theatrical
moving van (Schumer's), silver-colored long-distance
buses (Campus Coach Lines), suppliers' trucks (Thos. A.
Deming: platforms, tents, bleacher seats, chairs, tables),
limousines, and big green Hertz vans. Only a narrow and
uncertain lane was left in the middle of the street for
motorists traveling from Sixth Avenue to Fifth, and cars
trying to get in and out of the big parking garage directly
across from the Algonquin were having an even worse
time than they usually do. The entrance to the Algonquin
was hedged in with ropes and coils and boxes and tripods
and lights, and at the curb a red revolving light on a stand
about three feet high went round and round in a triumphant way that made me feel oppressed and obedient. I
was standing in a window of the hairdresser's on the second floor of the Royalton Hotel, across the street from the
Algonquin. I was having my hair done, and every once in a
while I struggled out from under the dryer and went to the
windows to have a look. I was not the only curious one. M.
Paul, who owns the establishment, and his assistant,
Pauline, who has blue-black hair and comes from Nor-
mandy, also kept going to the windows to look out. I asked
if she had ever seen Julie Andrews. "Not in person," she
said regretfully. The Royalton Hotel and the Algonquin
Hotel are about the same age, both of them going on

seventy — handsome, strong old places that are not at all alike except for the heavy Edwardian air they have, which is beginning to seem recalcitrant on this narrow street. The obliterating touch of the cement mixer is gradually smoothing this block into the bland expression that is the new New York. The street seems very close and at the same time quite distant from the Royalton windows, which are curtained only in a pale diaphanous material, a veil. Elizabeth Bowen once described a room that was crowded although there were no people in it as looking as if somebody were holding a party for furniture. The scene on Forty-fourth Street today looked as if somebody were holding a protest meeting for cars. There were very few people about, and nobody was standing and staring. The street would have been mobbed except that Miss Andrews and her caravan had come without fanfare into a very quiet weekend city. The doorman of the Algonquin kept hurrying out into the middle of the street, looking for taxis for people, but the rampart of trucks and vans hid most of what was going on. Once in a while we had a glimpse of the real movie people — the actors and actresses who made their headquarters in a very large silver omnibus that was parked in front of the Algonquin. The bus door opened, and a handsome, white-haired gentleman in evening clothes stepped down. He had handlebar mustaches and he wore a red carnation in his lapel, and he was carrying a cardboard box with coffee containers in it. A golden-haired lady in silver lamé climbed up into the bus.

Her dress was trimmed with silver fringe that undulated about her knees, and she wore a silver Pocahontas band around her head. At that moment, on Forty-fourth Street in her glittering stage dress, she was enviable and beautiful, part of the illusory world we all half hope to enter when we gather to watch the Hollywood people keep their enormous vigils on our streets. The golden-haired actress sat down in the front seat of the bus, across from the driver, and almost immediately bent her head and began making the gestures people make in airplanes when the stewardess has brought them their tray of food. She opened little envelopes and looked into them, and she opened big envelopes and looked into them, and then she began eating her box lunch. In the dim interior of the bus, she was only a shadow along with all the other shadows who sat eating or stood talking or walked to the bus door to step out into the daylight that showed them as they really were — costumed figures, the men in evening clothes, the girls dressed for a wild party of forty years ago. One of the bus seats was piled almost to the top of the window with light-colored, long-haired furs — furs of the nineteen-twenties. "It must be a movie about the twenties," M. Paul said. "Julie Andrews hasn't come out yet," Pauline said. When my hair was finished, I walked across to the Algonquin to buy cigarettes and have a look inside. At that early hour of the afternoon, even on a summer Saturday, there are always people sitting about the hotel, having a drink or reading the paper or waiting for friends to join them for lunch. Not today. The place looked half dismantled. The chairs and sofas were there, but there was no place for anybody to sit down, with all the movie clutter about and underfoot. The lobby, usually so comfortable and hospitable, looked like a setting for anxiety, and the Rose Room restaurant, at the end of the lobby, was drowned in a blaze of tall white lights that concentrated on the back wall and the bar. I picked my way across to the newsstand and bought cigarettes, and I was starting to leave when I saw Julie Andrews. She was alone, sitting in a high, high-backed armchair beside the entrance to the Rose Room, having her box lunch. Her tight short dress seemed to be made of crystal and light, and she was wearing a crystal headband for a crown; she looked like Titania. The chair was much too big and too high for her, and to balance herself and her lunch she had put her knees together, and her feet, balanced on the tips of her toes, were far apart. She was very hungry. All her attention was on her sandwich, which she picked up with both hands, and she was just about to take a bite out of it when she raised her eyes and saw me standing and staring at her. I immediately stopped thinking of Titania and began thinking of Lady Macbeth. At the sight of me, Julie Andrews froze in fury. Behind her sandwich, she was at bay, her hungry face glazed with anger. She is a Star, no doubt about that. She shines and radiates, and she can cast a spell, any kind of spell. Later in the afternoon, I went back to the Algonquin to get a taxi and first have another look around. This time, Julie Andrews was standing in the entrance to the hotel, having her photograph taken. Her flirtatious little dress shimmered mauve in the gray-white daylight, and she might have been the girl Scott Fitzgerald had in mind when he wrote:

> There'd be an orchestra
> Bingo! Bango!
> Playing for us
> To dance the tango,
> And people would clap
> When we arose
> At her sweet face
> And my new clothes.

I looked over at the Royalton, and beside Chez Paul's filmy curtains I saw a neat blue-black head. Pauline, catching a glimpse of Julie Andrews in person.

JUNE 17, 1967

The Sorry Joker

ONE night recently, in the Longchamps Restaurant at Madison Avenue and Fifty-ninth Street, I had the satisfaction of seeing a practical-joker type smacked down, and in such a way that he could do absolutely nothing to save his face. That night was rainy — a steady, heavy rain. I was having dinner in one of the crescent-shaped booths they have at Longchamps; it was one that faces the entrance door and the street window on the Madison Avenue side. It was about nine-thirty, and in the light from the street lamps and from the few shop windows that were still lighted the rain fell brightly, but hardly anybody passed by. It was too wet for walking that night. There were not many people in the big restaurant, and the long bar was quite deserted, but at a table by the door four people were sitting — two men and two women — and they were very noisy, laughing a lot and shouting at the waiter and changing their minds about what they wanted to eat. One of the men, the one who talked the loudest and the most, the life of the party, was sitting with his back to me, but I could see the faces of his three companions. When I had been there only a couple of minutes, the revolving door went around very slowly and a tall elderly lady wearing a transparent raincoat over her regular coat, and a transparent rain hat over her real hat, and transparent galoshes, came in, carrying a very wet umbrella. She opened her raincoat, and from inside it, where they had been keeping dry, she drew out a book and a folded newspaper that looked like the London *Times*. Then, without hesitation, she started to walk toward a table not far from me. But she had taken only a few paces past the table by the door when the man with his back to me turned his chair noisily and shouted "Hey, *lady!*" after her. The lady turned and took a step or two back toward him, and found him laughing senselessly, looking up at her, and his three companions convulsed with amusement at the sight of her startled face. She turned away from them immediately and again started walking to her table, and this time she reached it and sat down, but she forgot to take off her raincoat, which billowed out awkwardly around her, shining with raindrops. The waiter brought her a menu and then went to attend to someone else. She looked at the menu and laid it on the table and began to stare in the direction of the street, but her eyes kept wandering over to the four rude strangers by the door, who gave every sign of enjoying themselves and each other and their dinner. She took up the menu again, and then she put it back on the table and took up her book, her London *Times*, her handbag, her gloves, and her umbrella, and went out of the restaurant as quietly as she had come in, but in disarray. I was afraid that the man might speak to her again as she passed his table, but I do not think he saw her go. It had been a pointless little scene, but the point was that there had been a scene. Someone had been humiliated. A woman had been deprived of the quiet dinner she had promised herself, and now she was going to have to decide on another place and on how to get there in the rain, and she would probably decide to just give up and go home.

To divert myself from the spite I was feeling, I began to watch a fat lady in a pearly satin Nefertiti turban who sat a good distance off, several empty tables away from me, in the corner booth by the window. She was square and pink, all flesh, and she sat up very straight, with her back pushed firmly against the back of the booth, and her round dark eyes, like an idol's eyes, seemed to look directly at nothing. She hardly moved her head on its erect, portly neck, and as her eyes moved over the restaurant she seemed to see not one person, or two, but millions, maybe billions, of people, and she ate steadily. A man sat with her, but she never spoke to him. Her fork was in her right hand, and her right hand never rested; she was eating something creamy — chicken à la king, or something like that. Her left hand was laid against the base of her throat, flat against her skin, and the ring she wore sparkled brilliantly, like her earrings. When I first looked at her, she was lifting some food from her plate, and as she carefully raised the fork she glided her left hand down and placed it, palm downward, under the food, and so conducted the fork up to her face, in a gesture that looked as though she might be about to dance in Bali. When the food was safe, when she was eating it, the fork went down onto the plate again, and her left hand was laid back against her throat again until the fork could be filled once more. Her imperturbability and the smoothness and style of her gestures and the independence of her arms and the separate independence of her head made me believe that I was seeing how Siva might eat and still maintain an inhuman ascendancy, because the common work of eating detracted no more from the majesty of this woman in Longchamps than falling down a cliff detracts from the majesty of water or passing through clouds detracts from the majesty of the sun. She would remain the same, whatever she did. Nothing would affect her. Nothing could make her vulnerable or cause her shame or discomposure. No one would ever drive *her* out of the restaurant she had made up her mind to dine in.

I glanced over at the four rude people, and I was glad I did, because just then the joker fell off his chair. He did not slide off or slip off — there was no chance for him to pretend he was acting — he *fell* off and hit the floor with a fearful thump, and his chair fell over, too, with a small crash. His companions behaved abominably. They did not reach down to help him up, or chortle companionably at him, or anything like that. Instead, the second man in the party turned his back and began to watch the street, and the two women took their mirrors out of their handbags and gave critical attention to their forelocks. The Joker stayed sitting on the floor for perhaps half a minute, staring at the hem of the tablecloth, and then he got up and set the chair straight and began to blame the chair and said he would sue Longchamps. He shook the chair to show how it wobbled, but it was as solid as a rock, and he sat down on it and stopped talking. He drank some coffee. None of the others spoke. They seemed to feel that the fun had gone out of the evening. The second man waved for the check and signed for it, and they all went out into the rain.

I looked across at the Idol, because I wanted to know

how she placed her hands when she was not eating, but her dinner plate must have been bottomless — she was still at it. In my turn, I left the restaurant, and started looking for a taxi home, and the only regret I had was that the lady with the London *Times* had not stayed long enough to see her tormentor get his comeuppance.

JANUARY 20, 1962

Giving Money in the Street

IT is and always has been my inclination to give money to people who ask me for money on the street, and I always give something — usually a quarter these days, where I used to give a dime. I know people who say that to give money to someone who asks for it on the street is to submit to blackmail and that most of the people who ask on the street are frauds. I say that I would rather give the quarter and walk on free than not give it and pay out the rest of the day, or even an hour or ten minutes of the day, in doubt: should I have given it after all, the chances are surely fifty percent against the person's being a fraud, and so on. I find that a decision to do something leaves me free, while a decision not to do something only leaves me surrounded with undone things and endless, exasperating chances of changing my mind. Not long ago, I was going to a matinée with a friend and I had the tickets and I was late. I was to meet my friend at the theater. It was raining hard. I stood outside the Algonquin Hotel waiting for a taxi for about five minutes before I realized that even if a taxi came along it would be going the wrong way — it would be going east, and my theater was on Forty-fifth Street west of Broadway. I got across Sixth Avenue and walked very fast and made the light at the corner of Forty-fifth and got across, so that I was on the right side for the theater. Then I really tore along toward Broadway; I could go so fast because it was raining so hard that there was no one to get in my way. While I was hurrying along, I opened my bag and got out a dollar bill to have ready in case a taxi stopped and somebody got out, and when I got near Broadway I suddenly wondered if I really had the tickets, and I opened my bag again and looked in, and they were there, all right. I saw that the light at Broadway was red, and I thought that by the time I got to the corner it should be turning green and I would be able to race right across. Just then I saw, standing near the corner of Forty-fifth and Broadway, an unfortunate-looking woman who wore a straw hat and a little short black coat and who was holding a box top in her hands and looking toward me. I thought, That poor woman thinks I took something out of my bag to give her. Then I thought, I would have given the dollar to the taximan anyway and I'll just give it to her and maybe I'll get to the theater on time, and as I was going past her I put the dollar in the box top, which held two or three yellow pencils and some brown shoelaces. That took a second or so, and as I rushed on I heard her say, "Oh, it's

too much," but I did not stop, and then I heard her coming
after me crying "It's too much, it's too much." She caught
me at the corner just as I was stepping down into the
street, and I had to turn and speak to her, and I said several
times, "Oh, it's all right," but, of course, I couldn't take
time to talk about it, and she seemed agitated, so I took
back the dollar and tore across Broadway and left her
standing there in the rain. I didn't look around when I got
to the other side, and I was just in time at the theater, and
while my friend was watching the curtain go up and settling down to enjoy the afternoon I was wondering what a
dollar was too much *for.* Too much for me to give? I
suppose so. Too much for her to take? Why? She hadn't
tried to get me to take any, or all, of the few pencils and
shoelaces she had in the box top. I decided that a person
who invites money on the street and then wants to limit or
set the amount to be given *is* a fraud, but I feel I have not
finished with the matter yet, and I have an uneasy suspicion that the decision I make is going to go against me,
although I do not see why it should be so.

JULY 23, 1960

Bad Tiny

I HAVE just seen the worst-mannered dog in New York
City, and possibly in the world. Her name is Tiny,
and her mistress is blind, and from now on, whenever I see

one of those gentle Seeing Eye dogs that sit and lie for hours on end on the hot midsummer sidewalks up and down Fifth Avenue and on the side streets off the avenue, attending while their blind masters collect money for one purpose or another, I will think of Tiny and wish that she would take a moment to contemplate her colleagues and maybe learn a little about the source from which they draw the fortitude that saves their dignity in the face of acute discomfort and acute boredom.

I saw Tiny in the waiting room of the Ellin Prince Speyer Hospital for Animals, which is quite far downtown. I had to take a little cat there for treatment, and while I was waiting my turn to see the doctor, Tiny and her blind mistress came plunging into the room, accompanied by an old lady whose only function, as far as I could make out, was to repeat Tiny's name over and over again, in tones of reproach, admiration, and awe, so that we would all know who it was that we were looking at. Tiny's mistress, who was holding on to the harness with both hands, was very old indeed, and her temper was almost as bad as her dog's. Every time the companion tried to touch her elbow to guide her out of the laps of the people waiting on the benches, the old blind lady gave the companion a violent push, and it was at these moments that the companion would wail, "Tiny, Tiny," and it is possible that she was not speaking to the dog we were all being forced to look at but was recalling some nicer, smaller, thinner, more polite dog, who had perhaps been the current Tiny's predecessor in the fierce affections of the old blind lady. It was not hard to see that according to her mistress, the dog we were all pulling our legs and animals out of the way of could do no wrong. Tiny had "favorite" written all over her, and she looked as though she lived on chocolate creams. She was big and fat and curly, with a pointed nose and mean little eyes, and her bark was shocking. In the waiting room at Speyer, they have long benches where people sit, and when the benches are filled up, the late-comers stand. The benches were filled up that day, but several people got up to make room for this noisy trio, headed by Tiny, who continued to strain frantically at her harness even after the old ladies were seated. Tiny wanted to get out of the place. Apparently — the blind old lady began to talk after she had sat down — Tiny often visits the Speyer Hospital. She goes there to be weighed. They have her on a diet, and I suppose she associates these visits with fewer treats and smaller portions of food. All the other animals were scandalized by her bad manners. The other dogs — poodles and a collie and a beautiful Afghan — all kept looking down in embarrassment and looking away, and one small furry young dog just stared at her in astonishment. The cats, in their baskets, were as silent as they were invisible, but their contempt was in the air. One of the men who had surrendered his place on the bench was carrying a tiny monkey wrapped in a shawl, and the monkey seemed to be deliberately averting his damp, wistful eyes from the sight of the hysterical Tiny. The monkey was distressed to see a creature so full of ill will and bad temper. Everyone was distressed and silent to see a grown dog in a tantrum, and the room was terribly hot and crowded. Tiny and the two old ladies were ushered into the doctor's office as quickly as possible, and we were all glad to see them go. Soon we heard Tiny's voice again, making new dreadful sounds, which probably indicated she was being weighed.

Shortly afterward I took my little cat in to another of the offices, and I had to leave her there for treatment, so I walked out of the office alone. Outside the door of the waiting room at Speyer there is a forbidding-looking flight of stone steps — quite steep, wide steps — that leads down to the street doors. Side rails are there for people who might be afraid of slipping or tripping and falling all the way down to the bottom. As I left the waiting room, Tiny and her convoy hurtled out behind me, the companion crying, "Tiny, Tiny," and the old blind lady keeping her lips pressed tightly together, as seemed to be her habit when under way. Tiny made a murderous dash for the top of the steps and got her old mistress right to the edge, where she stood holding on to the harness with one hand and with the other hand feeling around for something that would guide her down the steps. But Tiny was pulling her away from the rail. The old lady was going to lose her balance, and then she would fall, and she would certainly be battered to death as Tiny dragged her down to the street. I grabbed a side rail with one hand, and with the other hand I grabbed the old lady's arm, hoping very much that I would not be dragged to destruction along with her. Little did I know, fool that I was. That old lady was as strong as an ox, and the next thing that happened, without even turning her beautiful snowy head in my direction she sent me spinning over to the rail with such force that if it had been a knife I would have been cut in half or, rather, into a third and two thirds, for I am a short person.

There is little left to tell. I skidded down the steps, holding on to the rail, and hurried out onto the street just in time to avoid being trampled under by that trio. I was lucky enough to find a taxi at once, and as I sailed away uptown, collecting myself, I caught a final glimpse of the three of them, trotting happily along, Tiny carrying her head up and wearing an air of genuine virtue and the two old ladies chatting amiably. Going home to tea and cake, I suppose. I could not help wondering, they made such an angelically serene picture walking together on a summer afternoon: What if they had knocked me down and left me crushed at the foot of those steps; who would have had the heart to tell them what they had done? Would anyone have wanted to run after them and capture them and accuse them? I cannot believe it. Nobody would have wanted to spoil their contentment with themselves and with each other. Nobody would be so cruel, and things are not always what they seem.

JULY 29, 1961

An Irritating Stranger

TODAY is Sunday, and an hour ago, in the hot August sun, I was standing by the fountain across from the Plaza Hotel feeding an expensive Plaza Hotel brioche to some pigeons, who were lethargic but were determined to have their rights, and to two thin sparrows, who knew they had no rights but were determined to get something to eat. I was on the side of the sparrows, but I did not want to antagonize the pigeons. I like pigeons. I cannot imagine where they get their pampered air, but they have it and I like them for having it. I stood there placating the pigeons and favoring the sparrows. I was throwing the crumbs cleverly and with real strategy when I heard a girl say, "I can see that New York might be a nice place to visit, and I suppose if you live here it's different." I listened, but she said no more. Her voice was cheerful and definite. I turned to look at her, and found that she was walking away toward the park, but I could see that she was the same red-haired girl I had been watching earlier from the Edwardian Room of the Plaza Hotel while I was having breakfast. The table I had been given was placed so that although I was not sitting by a window, I had a view out through a window on the Fifth Avenue side and through two windows on the Fifty-ninth Street side. Through the first window I saw the fountain and, beyond the fountain, the big buildings of Fifth Avenue, and through the other windows I saw Fifty-ninth Street, with the green park beyond. People appeared in one window and reappeared in another, moving slowly through the heat. It was all burning-dry summer, except for the shine of water from the fountain. When I first saw the red-haired girl, she was standing just where I later stood while I fed the birds, and she was taking a photograph of three men, who were lined up in front of her with their arms hanging at their sides, looking rather foolish and very obedient. I noticed her first when a sudden breeze lifted her hair, so that for a second or two it flared straight up in the air, showing its color, which was brilliant. Now I stood looking after her. I was fumbling with what she had said. There was only one man with her, and I wondered what had happened to the two others. Her remark, in all its vacancy, had begun to mope around in my mind, and it said nothing, and the more I looked at it the more it said nothing, and it wouldn't go away. It was a suffocating remark — the kind that makes you want to cry. One time, I knew somebody who always greeted me by saying, "Well, there you are! You know, I've been worried about you." I did not know that person very long. The red-haired girl crossed Fifty-ninth Street and went into the park, and I saw her no more.

That is a handsome and spacious intersection where Fifth Avenue and Fifty-ninth Street and the Plaza Hotel meet, but on ordinary days it is busy and noisy and full of strain. This morning, in the empty summertime, the streets and the park and the substantial Fifth Avenue buildings all stretched themselves out to their full length and full height and full bulk, and the Plaza sat there looking rich, and the whole scene was free and amiable and impromptu. The few people who were about wore light-colored summer clothes, and they sauntered and strolled and paused to look around like the extras in an operetta just before the principals walk on and take the center of the stage. At that moment, from where I stood feeding the birds, the center of the stage was taken by the line of patient horses, one of them a lovely piebald, who stood harnessed to their canopied carriages, waiting with their masters for the customers. It was a nice Sunday morning in New York. That red-haired girl had a carefree walk. If she was miserable, why did she not droop and go somewhere else and shut up?

Beyond the horses, over there where the girl and her companion had disappeared, I had seen four women in loose flowered dresses pass by earlier, as I sat in the restaurant. They walked steadily along, and they seemed eager to get where they were going, and oblivious of the street and the park and of everything except whatever occasion was ahead of them, but they were not hurrying. They had allowed plenty of time. They appeared in one window, walking along by the low park wall, and then they disappeared and appeared again in the next window, still making good time. The windows in the Plaza are immense and impressively overdressed in miles and miles of heavy tasseled hangings and in pounds of shirred beige blinds. It is a good, big, solidly theatrical room, and this morning it was about half full of strangers having a late, leisurely Sunday-morning breakfast. The atmosphere was very sedate. Nobody waved at anybody across the room. None of the people coming in stopped at a table to say hello. There were no nods or smiles of recognition. The room was all transients who were there for breakfast, and that was that. The Sunday *Times* was divided up at every table where two or more people sat together, and where one person sat alone the *Times* was piled neatly on a chair while the chosen section was being read. The woman at the table next to me was devoting herself seriously to the Review of the Week section. My view of Fifty-ninth Street was crosswise, over her shoulder. She was wearing a tailored black silk suit. Her hair was drawn back in a small bun, and in the bun she had anchored a number of silver pins, and from every pin a heavily chased silver bead hung free and wobbled. A silver fish, three inches long, dangled from each of her ears. I looked past her at the four walking women outside. Three of them were quite tall and upright, but the fourth, who walked on the edge of the sidewalk, along by the curb, was very small and bent, and she did not walk, she toddled. The three others were bareheaded, but she had a cotton scarf tied over her hair and under her chin, and she held on to the arm of the woman next to her and followed trustfully along, with her head down, keeping all her attention to herself, as though she were concentrating on the labor of walking and of listening to what the

younger women were saying. The younger women might
have been grandmothers, and she was old enough to be a
great-great-grandmother. Her dress covered her ankles.
They all looked happy, and the very old woman looked as
though she knew she was in good hands. She looked
content. She was going somewhere. She was having an
outing. Not one of them even bothered to turn her head as
they passed by the park and the park entrance. They only
looked up and down Fifth Avenue, because of the traffic
there, and when they reached the sidewalk that started
them toward the east side of the city they all marched
forward along Fifty-ninth as though they would be will-
ing to walk as far as the river if what they wanted was to be
found there.

The silver fish in my neighbor's ears were no longer idle.
They were dancing around, up and down, swinging here
and there. There was a reason for their activity. Their
owner was eating her breakfast melon. She was taking
enormous spoonfuls out of the melon, a big, wide wedge
of honeydew, and she was still reading hard. She had
folded the paper in a businesslike way, so that only the
columns that concerned her showed, and she held it upright in her strong left hand. Suddenly she put her spoon
down and looked intently at the melon, and then she put
the *Times* down and began to search with her head for a
waiter. She turned so that I saw her face. She looked
wild-eyed but in control, as though the train were about to
leave and the porter had not yet arrived with her luggage.

The room was full of waiters, and one came immediately. He listened to what she had to say, and while he was listening the headwaiter came and listened too. The waiter looked worried, but the headwaiter only smiled understandingly. Apparently the melon she had been given was very poor. She must have been too interested in her reading to notice how awful it was, because she had eaten a great deal of it. She said many things, and when she stopped talking the waiter took the melon away and brought another big wedge and placed it before her. This time the headwaiter stood by and watched attentively while she took the first spoonful, and while she was tasting it, before she had swallowed it, she looked at him, smiling and nodding, and then she raised her right hand high in the air and made a circle with her thumb and forefinger, saluting the melon and the headwaiter and, I suppose, herself and the Plaza Hotel. Was she splendidly unselfconscious, or was she ridiculous? I didn't know. I was tired of her.

My waiter brought my change, and I took the leftover brioche and got up and left and went to stand beside the fountain to feed the pigeons and, as it turned out, two sparrows, and, as it turned out, to hear that red-haired girl drop her empty remark. That was about an hour ago. She is probably still strolling around Central Park, carrying her camera and saying things. I wonder who is listening to her now. I am glad I am not.

SEPTEMBER 1, 1962

The Cheating of Philippe

I AM one of those morning-newspaper readers who turn first to the obituary page. If I see that someone I know — someone I have heard of, even — is dead, I am astonished, and usually sorry. If I see no name that is familiar to me, I am relieved, or even glad, and I suppose it is in order to atone for this increased sense of life, which comes to me as a free gift from the daily lists of the unknown dead, that I always give my complete attention to reading through the accounts of their lives, and always look at their photographs, and I can hardly bear it if they are smiling. It may be curiosity that drives me to the obituary pages, but the impulse behind that curiosity — if it is curiosity — is far more interesting and mysterious than the curiosity itself, and I might talk for a long time before I could reach the truth of it, and I might never reach the truth of it, and at the moment I have to continue, because I am all taken up with the story of a stranger, a restaurant keeper, who died this past summer and whose obituary I do *not* remember seeing in the pages of the morning newspaper. His name was Philippe. The restaurant that was his domain is in a lovely block in the East Sixties, and it has one of those comfortable, promising names, like La Belle Poire or Le Chat Extraordinaire, that remind you of seventeen or thirty-seven other good French restaurants in the city and make you think that it is time to revisit your favorite among them. I never saw

Philippe, and I had never heard of his restaurant until one
fine evening in the middle of August, when I was wandering around after looking at apartments and suddenly became aware that in this particularly cozy block of small art
galleries and antique shops and dress shops there was a
small French restaurant, and that it was open — then, at
that time of year, when almost all the restaurants that you
want to go to are closed for a long vacation. I had already
passed it while I was looking at it, and I turned back and
took a good look. It seemed to be a very small restaurant,
and it looked very welcoming. I went in. It was a few
minutes past six, and they had only just opened the place
for the evening. The room was cool and dim after the
warmth and brightness outside, and the tables were all
dressed up and festive, and there were flowers here and
there and a shine of color from the bottles over the bar at
the back, but it was empty — no customers. There were
five or six waiters standing talking, and when I came in
they looked at me with surprise and expectancy, as though
they were certain I must be, or could only be, the herald of
a great rush of customers. There was a time when I used to
feel uneasy about taking up a table all to myself in a
restaurant, but I have improved since then, and so I
quickly informed the waiters that I was only what I appeared to be, one person, and then I refused the table they
offered me, and sat down at another one, just as good. Two
waiters, who may or may not have been aware of my small
triumph, hurried over, and one of them handed me an

enormous menu and the other poured a great deal of water into my water goblet. I began to read the menu, and in a minute or two a small man in black, the host, hurried in from the kitchen or wherever he had been and asked me politely if I would like a drink. I said yes, and what. Then I ordered dinner. Then I took out the book that I generally carry with me in my handbag, because it diverts me when there is nothing to listen to and camouflages my eavesdropping when there is something to listen to, and I began to read. A good while passed — I had nearly finished dinner — and then another customer came in, a man by himself. This time the host was on the spot, and he greeted the new man with a smile and with words of recognition and joy and showed him to a table that was close to mine. The man looked very much at home, and he nodded across the room to all the waiters and glanced about the place as though he knew it well. Then he leaned forward to look back down the room and past the bar toward the kitchen.

"Where's Philippe?" he asked. "I ran into a friend of his in Edinburgh this summer."

The host stopped smiling at once. "Oh, Monsieur," he said, "Philippe is no longer with us."

Now the customer stopped smiling. "No longer *with* you?" he said, almost shouting.

The host looked wretchedly nervous, and he hesitated, "You see," he said, "Philippe passed away this summer."

There was some murmuring between them that I could

not catch, and after that the guest said, almost rudely, "All right, then, I'll have a Rob Roy. A *sweet* Rob Roy." He began to read the menu with great care, holding it close to his face, and when the drink came he reached around the menu for it and began to drink it behind the menu, almost with secrecy, as though he were ashamed of himself. He ordered dinner with no enthusiasm, and I felt very sorry for him, and even more sorry for Philippe, who must have loved his restaurant and would have been dismayed to know that he was now only a ghost at his own feast.

I left the restaurant then and thought no more about it until a few nights ago, when I remembered how nice it was and went over there for dinner. I arrived just before seven, and there were quite a lot of tables occupied and more people drifting in all the time, and again and again I saw the little host go through the same gloomy explanation that he had given before about Philippe. Many of the people who were coming in were obviously old customers. The host hurried hospitably forward to greet each of the new arrivals, but it was easy to see that although he was glad to see them, he also dreaded seeing them. In the period since my first visit there, Philippe had passed from being a distressing ghost to being the skeleton who rattles and will not get into the cupboard and be still. I was sorry about that. I thought it might have been a good idea for Philippe's colleagues to greet every returning old customer with a glass of champagne in which to toast their dead friend, but since this was not done, I can only hope that

Philippe's long and dreary wake will soon be over. I think he would have hated it. I hope that his next incarnation, when his bones cease their rattling, will be amid pleasant things that would have been familiar to him, amid sounds — the sounds of a prosperous and friendly restaurant at its best hour, the sounds from the kitchen when it is busiest, and the sounds of corks being drawn from bottles and of ice being shaken and of knives and forks and of waiters' questioning voices and of customers in cheerful conversation over a good dinner, sounds that we all know and that signify perhaps the most amiable moments of our days, wherever we are, or, as we all happen to be, in the midst of life.

DECEMBER 31, 1960

West Eighth Street Has Changed and Changed and Changed Again

THE view from the University Restaurant, on West Eighth Street, has changed and changed and changed again since the beginning of July, when they began tearing down three small gray apartment houses across the street. One afternoon I walked toward the restaurant from Fifth Avenue and did not notice the houses; they had always been there, and were so familiar as to be invisible. The next afternoon they were completely visible,

because workmen were taking out the windows and had
already laid a ramp of doors across the sidewalk. The three
houses came down quite fast, considering how solid they
looked, and how settled and comfortable in their place —
next to the Whitney Museum, that lovely house that is
now a youth center. As her doomed neighbors came tumbling down — no dignity, all secrets exposed — the
Whitney huddled more and more into herself, like a poor
old woman pulling her shawl around her shoulders in
wintertime. "I may not be what I used to be," the Whitney
seemed to be saying, "but I don't want to go just yet." The
three gray houses did not want to go, either, but they went
anyway, with their thick walls and their good floors and
their strong staircases and their many-colored rooms and
all their windows — the ordinary square ones and the
high-up skylights. Everything ended up down on the
ground and was carted off, and what was left was what
must have been there originally — a clear view of the
backs of the tiny houses on the north side of Macdougal
Alley. Mr. Gregory, the proprietor of the University Restaurant, watched the destruction, day by day, with a sort of
unemotional disgust. "We had a lot of customers from
those apartments," he said. "A lot of teachers lived there.
But the Whitney — that was a wonderful house! A lot of
people from the Whitney used to come here when it was a
gallery — a lot of the visitors, and a lot of the people who
worked there." For Mr. Gregory, the abandonment of the
Whitney house as a museum was the *worst*, and it is from

that event that he dates the decline of West Eighth Street
from a Pleasant Place into a Wild Place.

For me, the *worst* was the day Mr. Joseph Kling packed
up his International Book & Art Shop, four doors east of
the restaurant, and moved two blocks or so west, to
Greenwich Avenue, because he couldn't afford the new,
high Eighth Street rents. Mr. Kling's shop was below
street level, directly across from the three houses that have
just come down. When a customer entered, Mr. Kling
used to emerge from the gloomy recesses at the far end of
his shop wearing a green eyeshade and an expression that
was sometimes menacing and sometimes merely distrust-
ful. The shop was long and narrow, with simple shelves
that went on and on to the far end, where a jumble and a
clutter suddenly occurred, as though the leftover books
had had to scramble for their places and were hanging on
to the wall for dear life. All down the center of the room,
plain wooden tables held maps and prints and photographs and more books. It was a dingy, stubborn, interesting place, and when Mr. Kling walked into view from his
lair at the back, the shop took on the haunted air that all
true secondhand bookshops have, all over the world. He
knew his books, and the books showed that he knew them
— there was not a foot of shelf in that shop where the eye
would slide along and away without finding something to
look at. You could spend hours there without wasting a
minute. Even if you bought nothing, you came out much
better off than you were when you went in. One night in
the winter of 1944, I walked in there quite late in the

evening — about nine o'clock. It was terribly cold. That was my fourth winter in New York City, and I still could not get used to the freezing winds that tore along the streets and never seemed to stop blowing. I thought the towering concrete canyons of the middle of Manhattan, where I was working, served to funnel and strengthen the fury of the winds, but even in the Village, where at that time the majority of the buildings were still low, the winds seemed to proceed from a hard ferocity that had nothing in common with ordinary weather or with ordinary times. It was too cold. I was living in one enormous room at the top of a beautiful house on East Tenth Street, just off Fifth Avenue, a few steps from the Grosvenor Hotel. I was six flights up, and my front wall was all windows — a solid row of casement windows looking south. At that time, as I said, the Village was still mostly not built up, and I had a long view of rooftops and chimney pots that even the most critical Parisian would have to admire — rooftops, roof gardens, terraces, studios, and a huge and always changing sweep of sky. But that winter the friendly expanse of rooftops turned into a flat and heartless plain across which the winds raced toward my casement windows; my casement windows had wooden frames and were very old, cracked, and warped, and offered little more protection than a canvas tent. And something had happened to the furnace in the house. For weeks we had no heat and no hot water. Finally, one night, I put on two coats and went out to walk about. There were very few people on the streets. Around nine o'clock, I walked into the International Book & Art Shop. It wasn't warm there, but it was warmer than my rooftop apartment. Mr. Kling peered out from his corner at the back but did not come forward, and I made my way peacefully down the shop until I got to where he sat talking with a friend. They stopped talking and looked at me, and I imagined there was a question in the air. "My apartment is so cold I couldn't stay there," I said. "I had to come out. Even the streets seem warmer than the house I am living in." The friend said, "It is the kind of weather that makes people get married." Mr. Kling said nothing for a minute, and then he laughed grimly and said, "Berlin, 1923."

Berlin, 1923. New York City, 1944. And now it is New York City in the autumn of 1966. We are having Indian summer, and a sunny haze hangs over the trees in Washington Square. Tall, frail-looking, boxy new apartment houses confront each other flatly across lower Fifth Avenue, but the shape of the avenue — the marvelous sweep from Washington Square Arch straight uptown and into the far distance — remains unchanged. Over on Greenwich Avenue, Mr. Kling is still in business, still wearing his green eyeshade and his two expressions. The Grosvenor Hotel has been turned into a student residence, and the Brevoort and the Lafayette and the Holley are gone, but the small Hotel Earle, shabby and elegant, still holds the place it has held for more than sixty years at the corner of Waverly Place and Macdougal Street, and the Albert looks romantic and foreign at night when the lights go on in the dining room and in the bar and over the sidewalk

café. The Albert is on University Place between Tenth and
Eleventh streets, and Thomas Wolfe used to live there.
This is a very autumnal Indian summer, and in the cool
sunlight the side streets off Fifth and the winding Village
streets to the west and south are filled with dreams and
shadows, and there seems to be room for everyone. I am
sitting by the street window of the University Restaurant,
looking out at the dark blue wooden paling that hides the
empty place where those gray apartment houses were. Mr.
Gregory, at his desk, seems to be intoning a litany in his
gravelly voice, but he is only dictating the menus for tomorrow's lunch and tomorrow's dinner to his printer over
the telephone. "Russian shashlik," Mr. Gregory says, and
then he says, "Ham steak." It was in July 1941, when I was
a visitor to New York, that I first walked into this restaurant and ordered a dinner of lamb chops. Now, in the hazy
afternoon, I eat broiled bluefish and mashed potatoes, and
I look across the street at the dark blue paling and at the
shuddering specter of the long-gone Whitney Museum,
and I think: What next? What next?

NOVEMBER 12, 1966

Ludvík Vaculík

"THE truth is not in triumphing. It is merely what
remains when everything else has been squandered
away." "This spring has just ended and will never return.

Everything will be known in the winter." These are the words of a Czech writer, Ludvík Vaculík, and they are taken from his "Manifesto of Two Thousand Words," which was published in several Czech newspapers last June, at a time when Czechoslovakia was jubilant. The "Manifesto" was signed by over seventy Czechs — "from sports to science, Communist and non-Communist," according to Jerry Landay, a news commentator on station WINS, who has recently returned from Prague. Mr. Landay talked about the "Manifesto" and read excerpts from it on WINS at intervals from about midnight until dawn Wednesday, August 21, when we in New York had just heard of the invasion of Czechoslovakia by the Russians. WINS is an all-news station, and we were told that tanks were moving through the streets of Prague, and that the Central Committee building and Radio Prague were being surrounded, and that Alexander Dubček and other high government officials had been taken away, their destination unknown, and over and over again we were told that "some Czech citizens are trying to stop advancing Russian tanks with their bodies." And from time to time Mr. Landay would repeat his speech, telling us that he had returned from Prague with a souvenir he values highly — six pieces of paper containing an English translation of Mr. Vaculík's "Manifesto." The "Manifesto" was not authorized by the Dubček government, but neither did the government forbid or suppress it. Each time Mr. Landay spoke of the "Manifesto" and its signatories, he said the same thing: "It was both the vibrant symbol of Czech rebirth — its unofficial Declaration of Independence — and suddenly its Last Will and Testament." While I listened to WINS, I looked through the city edition of the *New York Times,* which had gone to press just as the first bulletins of disaster came from Prague. There were three-column headlines on the front page saying, "PRAGUE REPORTS INVASION BY TROOPS OF THE SOVIET, POLAND AND EAST GERMANY," and the story that followed gave all the news that was available up to about ten-thirty. I read all of that issue of the *Times* — all about the Democrats getting ready for their Convention, all about everybody. I read about the Londoner who saved his pet goldfish, George, from drowning and may receive an award from the Royal Society for the Prevention of Cruelty to Animals for his act. And I read about another Londoner, a cleaning lady in St. Alban's Cathedral, who picked up a rumpled brown paper bag from under one of the pews and found inside not the stale sandwiches she expected but seventy-five hundred dollars' worth of gold and platinum, diamonds, bloodstones, and onyxes — a dazzling haul. On page 2 of the *Times* there was a photograph of Count Carl-Gustav von Rosen, the Swedish aviator who broke the Nigerian blockade of Biafra and got food in to the starving Biafran people. And on page 3 there was a photograph I kept turning back to look at, because I thought the two faces shown there reflected the spirit of Ludvík Vaculík's words. It was a photograph of two white South African students standing still with their heads up while other white students threw white paint at them. According to the *Times*, a group of students drove thirty miles from Witwatersrand University to Prime Minister Vorster's residence in Pretoria to present a petition protesting a government veto of the appointment of a black African social anthropologist to a lecturing post at Capetown University. The two photographed are nineteen or twenty years old, and they have conventional haircuts — boys' haircuts — and they are wearing conventional suits. One of them has on a shirt and tie under his jacket, but the other is so covered with paint that it is hard to tell if he is wearing a tie or not. In any case, they put on good clothes for the occasion of presenting the petition, and their clothes are ruined. They stand with their hands down — holding books, I think — and the only sign they give of self-defense is to half close their eyes. Their faces are grim but not angry or distressed, and they look as though they were standing their ground not for the present only but also for the future. There was a lot to read in that copy of the *Times*, while I listened to WINS and Jerry Landay, but I kept turning back to the two South African boys.

Dawn came about six — a thick, dark orange dawn that cleared slowly to show the morning sky pale and unenthusiastic over the city. As soon as it was full light, I started over to Seventy-fourth Street and Second Avenue. I wanted to see if any kind of early-morning service was being held at the Jan Hus Presbyterian Church there, but

no one was around or near the church except one man
sitting on the front steps reading a newspaper. I walked a
bit. That is a wide-open, airy section of the city, close to
the river, with the usual tall, new, balconied apartment
houses looking very clean and big next to the older buildings, smaller, darker, and out of fashion. There were numbers of people out, all of them walking dogs, but First
Avenue is wide and free-looking, and there is little traffic
there at that hour — seven-fifteen or so — and the dogs
and their owners looked natural and happy, as though they
were in the city because they enjoyed it, not because they
had to be here. At one time the Czech and Slovak citizens
of New York were concentrated in the area from Seventy-
first to Seventy-fifth Street, and there are still many Czech
and Slovak restaurants and shops, a Czech funeral home,
Czech and Slovak names everywhere. In the doorway of a
tiny Czech gift shop, the proprietor stood reading the
Times, but except for the expression on his face, there was
no sign around that a blow had been struck that might
smash the globe and would in any case leave deep and
lengthening fissures in it. My walk took me past the Jan
Hus Presbyterian Church again. The man with the newspaper still sat there alone, engrossed in his reading. I took
a taxi to Fifty-sixth Street and Fifth Avenue and walked
downtown from there. It was getting on to eight o'clock,
and there were people walking along the street, walking to
work — a peaceful big-city scene, dominated by St. Pat-
rick's Cathedral on the east side of the avenue and Rocke-

feller Center on the west side. A thin, dark young man hurried past me reading a French-language newspaper that had headlines about the Russians and the Czechs. When I got to the corner of Forty-fourth and Fifth, I looked along the block and saw, way at the end, a little crowd of people gathered around the window of the Hammond Organ store, looking in. I thought: The organ people have put a television set in their window, and everybody is looking at the news from Prague. I hurried along to join them and made a place for myself between two distinguished-looking men, one black, one pinky white, both dressed for the day in neat business suits. Being short, I had to forage for my view, and when I finally got a look through the window I saw no television set but only a gray-haired lady sitting by a large organ and smiling out above our heads at something. I turned, and in front of the luncheonette across the street was a tall camera, and then I saw the familiar moviemaking truck — one truck only. They were making a movie. I turned back and stared in at the lady again. Not for long. A tall young man with black, curly hair came across the street and asked us to move away to the side — not all of us, only some. Apparently, a few of those at the window were bona fide members of the acting company. The two distinguished-looking men and I moved away and formed up again in a row on the sidewalk, where we stood staring at the curly-haired man, who did not seem pleased with us. "Farther back," he said patiently. "Move back, please. Back to the door, *please.*"

The three of us hurried to move about ten yards farther back, and when we had formed up again, our director was crossing the street, returning to his camera and its crew. We all suddenly realized whatever it was we realized, and we scattered hastily, going our different ways.

I went into the Algonquin Hotel and bought a copy of the late city edition of the *Times* and sat down and began comparing it with my well-worn early edition. In the late edition the Czechoslovakian news had headlines all across the front page, and took up so much space that many items that had been front-paged earlier had been pushed to the back pages, where they, in turn, displaced other items, including the one about George the goldfish and the one about the St. Alban's Cathedral cleaning lady. But Count Carl-Gustav von Rosen still turned an interested face to the world on page 2, and the South African students held their place on page 3, and their faces still reflected the prophetic challenge of Ludvík Vaculík's words. I would like to propose a cheer for the South African students and a cheer for Count Carl-Gustav von Rosen. A cheer for Jerry Landay. A cheer for the *New York Times*. A cheer for little George, whose life was saved by his kind and nimble master, Mr. Peter Humphrey, fifty-five. A cheer for the cleaning lady, Mrs. Ivy Rickman, who said of the bag of jewels, "My eyes popped out. I knew I'd have to tell a cathedral official, but I couldn't resist first trying on a few rings and bracelets." No cheers for Ludvík Vaculík. I ask God to bless him and keep him safe to write in freedom soon again. "This spring has just ended and will never return. Everything will be known in the winter."

SEPTEMBER 7, 1968

The Name of Minnie Smith

I HAD an early dinner last night on the second floor of the Schrafft's on Fifth Avenue at Forty-sixth Street. When I had nearly finished, two ladies came in and took the table next to mine. They both wore very large hats and had a great many strands of pearls around their necks, and I could not help hearing every word they said, because they talked very loudly. They both owned dress shops (or perhaps they only managed them; I couldn't be sure), and they had just come from a fashion showing on Seventh Avenue, and they had once worked together in the same dress house, but until this meeting, which was now ending with dinner at Schrafft's, they had not seen each other for several years. They mentioned the names of a good many people they both knew, and each name was ticked off with a remark or two that defined the absent one's achievement or lack of it — she had married or she had not married, she was divorced, she had or had not moved away from New York, she had gone into business for herself or she had failed in business and was now working for somebody, and so on. The names clattered between the two ladies,

and I had the feeling that everyone in the world was of the
same size and of the same unimportance, and that we
would all be disposed of very easily if these two women
ever got hold of our names. The girl had brought my
check and I was counting out my money when another
name was mentioned, and I shall say that the name was
Minnie Smith. Both ladies were eager talkers, but the
more eager one said, "Oh, Minnie Smith. Nice little
woman. Counts for nothing." Then she dropped a new
name, but I heard no more, because I was on my way to
the cash register to pay what I owed. I rode down to the
street floor in Schrafft's majestic elevator, and I walked out
onto Fifth Avenue and up Fifth to Forty-ninth and along
Forty-ninth to the hotel where I live, which is very close to
Seventh Avenue. On my way, I passed a lot of people, of
all sizes and shapes and colors and ages. I passed American soldiers and foreign sailors and delivery boys and
waiters and office workers and very young girls in groups
and very young boys in groups and fathers and mothers
and aunts and uncles and gypsies and bootblacks and
priests and policemen and taximen and highly dressed
people off for an evening on Broadway. Did I pass Minnie
Smith? I shall never know. I kept thinking, Oh, Minnie
Smith, what did you do to that awful woman? All the
other names were dropped and squashed and left to kick
themselves to death, but the name of Minnie Smith had
to be obliterated, and in the obliteration she was deline-
ated, and there she is now, larger than life. Imagine the

power of Minnie Smith, who counts for nothing and is not there and can still turn the spade they are digging her grave with into a flag with her name on it. I do not expect ever to see the two ladies from Schrafft's again, and so there is very little chance that I will ever have another glimpse into the very eager one's disappointed heart, where names are arranged according to the degree of the grudge that is held against them, but one thing I am certain of — on that ever-lengthening roster, the name of Minnie Smith leads all the rest.

AUGUST 31, 1963

Howard's Apartment

I AM back in the Village again, spending a few days in the apartment of a friend who is in London. The apartment is small, orderly, and individual — a one-person place that has remained aloof (friendly but aloof) since I walked in here with my suitcase on Thursday. "We have no secrets," the two little rooms seem to say, "but we are *his*." And I think that when I leave, the day after tomorrow, the same toy voice, whispering out of the walls, will cry, "What has been going on here? Who has been sitting in my chair? Who has been sleeping in my bed?" I know that voice. It is familiar to me, as it is to anyone who lives alone. It is the voice of the Three Bears, echoing one another — the Big Bear, the Smaller Bear, and the Smallest Bear. They start whispering when I open my own front door after I have been away awhile, after I have left my place to itself overnight, or for a week or a month. "Who has been at my kitchen? Who has been reading my books? Who has been touching my things?" The alarm in the Bears' voices is produced when they put their heads together to prove that they are thinking, and that they are aware, and that they are not sleepy, trusting fools but alert, knowledgeable Bears who know their way around in the world. (In fact, the Bears do not know their way around in the world, and they know that, but do other people know they know that?) At any excuse, they shoulder their cardboard guns and challenge the Darkness. "Who goes there?" "A Friend." "Pass, Friend." But wait a minute. "Who goes there?" "A Foe." "Pass, Foe." Friend or foe, what does it matter? The Bears have taken their stand, and, very much satisfied with themselves, they go back to sleep.

My friend's apartment is on Tenth Street between Fifth and Sixth, on the third floor of a brownstone that would delight its architect if he could come back to life to see how serenely his work has weathered the years. This is the rear apartment, and the people in front are giving a party. It is almost six now, and for the past hour I have been hearing their guests come up the stairs. Just as the new arrivals reach the landing, the door next to mine opens and there are shouts of greeting and breathless complaints in

male and female voices about the long climb up, and then
the door closes again on the party and the party noises.
The door is closed now, but there is a new sound. We had
a cloudburst a minute ago, or maybe it was only a few
seconds ago. The rain poured down. There was sudden
thunder, and lightning, and the sky, which had been white,
turned black. When the rain reached its full force, which
was immediately after it started to fall, the blue wood floor
of the terrace outside these living-room windows vanished
under a surprised azure mist as millions of drops of water
suddenly hit the boards and bounced back before falling
down forever. The big, humble sheepdog of an ailanthus
tree that leans its shoulders against the terrace became
soaked at once and bowed all its heavy heads in its eternal
submission to man's low opinion of it. The rain made a
great noise, but the rose bushes that edge the terrace held
themselves calmly up under the violence, and their leaves
fluttered in the rush of clean new air. As the rose leaves
fluttered, welcoming the downpour, the ailanthus trem-
bled all over, and the flat red-and-black side of a large
apartment building half a block away shone with color.
Wherever the rain fell there was color, and the rain fell
everywhere. At the first moment of the storm, when the
lightning flashed and the rain came thundering down, I
stood up from the green velvet sofa where I am sitting and
walked across to close the door to the terrace, and when I
turned back, the room had become dim — nothing left of
the brightness that had filled it all day. Now the room is

vague and insubstantial, and shows itself for what it really is — the accidental setting of an enigmatic but not disquieting dream that I have dreamed before, in past rooms, and will dream again, in rooms I have not yet seen. It is a dream without people. The rain has gathered the room and me into the invisible world where there is no night and no day, and where walls and mirrors and trees and bridges are formed of advancing and retreating sound. At this moment it is easy to see how mountains and oceans are created and erased by a shift in the light, and to understand that the solid earth may shrink without warning to the vanishing point underneath our feet. The rain falls steeply, making cliffs as it falls, and its force has turned this room into a cave that is real only because it is hollow — a sounding place in which there is only one sound. In the profound silence that rises here now, even echo and memory fade away.

At the moment when I stood up to close the terrace door, the people in the front apartment must have hurried to close their windows. They have no terrace. Their windows look out on Tenth Street, which is quite narrow, and across at a row of houses that share a long iron balcony — a straight tier of openwork iron, like a foreign postmark across their fronts. Every year the people who live along the balcony can see a miracle on this side of the street, on this house, where a vigorous old wisteria embraces the front wall from the sidewalk to the roof. When it is ready to bloom, the wisteria turns to face the world, offering itself to our eyes with all its strength. Only the sparrows flying up and down the wall can describe the wisteria in full bloom, as they touch it here and there, showing how their perch and refuge has become a tall cloud of purple and green that billows around and above the entrance and then flows royally up the front of the house from earth to sky. Mr. Ainsworth, who owns this house, lives downstairs, and he regards his big ailanthus tree and his big wisteria as his pets. Anyone seeing him look at them knows he would love to bring them both in every night, maybe even take them for a walk sometimes. He cares for them with fierce devotion, leaning far out of the high front windows and much too far out over the edge of this terrace, watching for the first sign of malaise in the tenacious, bony vines of his wisteria, or in the leaves and branches of his ailanthus. The ailanthus is fortunate, and the wisteria is fortunate, too, and so is this house — fortunate and well loved.

The rain is falling fast and as black as ever. The windows of the front apartment where the party is must be streaming with rain — frothing, almost — and Tenth Street must be streaming, too, and frothing black. But a cocktail party has to expand, if it can, and now the people in front have opened their door and left it open. What a lot of noise they are making with glasses and bottles and music and voices! They must have hundreds of people in there. Once in a while, over the low roar of conversation, there is a loud laugh, and once in a while a little shriek. Outside, all the noise in the world is being hammered into the earth

by the rain, and, inside, all the noise there is is effervescing
at the cocktail party. Only in this room there is stillness,
and the stillness has gone tense. The room is waiting for
something to happen. I could light the fire, but my friend
forgot to leave me any logs. I could turn on a lamp, but
there is no animal feeling in electricity. I stand up again
and walk over to the phonograph and switch it on without
changing the record that I played this morning. The music
strengthens and moves about, catching the pictures, the
books, and the discolored white marble mantelpiece as
firelight might have done. Now the place is no longer a
cave but a room with walls that listen in peace. I hear the
music and I watch the voice. I can see it. It is a voice to
follow with your mind's eye. *"La Brave, c'est elle."* There is
no other. Billie Holiday is singing.

NOVEMBER 11, 1967

POSTSCRIPT

The Last Days of New York City

I BORROW detective stories from a very small lending
library at the back of one of the many gift-and-card
shops that now crowd the Village streets. Last night, not
being able to find a book, I stared around at the shelves of
handwoven baskets, modern china, ceramic ashtrays, and
so on, and I saw a house made of playing cards but standing very solidly, because the cards were slit so that they
fitted together. I bought a pack of the cards, and then I
continued on home to the hotel on Washington Square
where I live at present. I have two rooms, eight floors up.
A clumsy iron balcony, beloved of pigeons, is built close up
against the windows so that it cuts off most of the view. It
was a lovely clear evening, and I climbed out onto the
balcony to take a look at the scene that it denied me.

There, eight stories down, was Washington Square. The
sidewalks that bound the park, the paths that flow north,
south, east, and west from the fountain to join the sidewalks, and the benches at the edge of the grass all were

crowded. On the corner diagonally across from me, an ice-cream man had anchored his cart — a square white cart, with a tall umbrella upright and full-blown in stripes of red and yellow. Not far from the ice-cream cart but on the grass, a woman stood alone, tossing her arms about. She might have been having a fit or placing a curse by her gestures, but there was a great commotion of pigeons around her, and I judged that she was feeding them, or that she had fed them and was explaining that the crumb bag was empty. A minute later the pigeons rose up in a crowd and swooped off between the trees. The woman walked away.

I heard lately — it is only a rumor, I suppose — that there is talk of cutting an underpass through Washington Square. I suppose that means that part of the square, anyway, will be dug up. It will hardly look the same after that.

When I first came to New York, I lived for a while at the Holley Hotel, on the west side of the square. The Holley was torn down this year, and lately, when I pass that way, I see the narrow gap — surprisingly narrow — where the little old hotel used to crouch between its tall apartment-building neighbors. At the time I lived there, only twelve years ago, a row of worn-looking studio buildings stretched partway across the south side of the Square. I thought those buildings were beautiful and romantic, and I used to long for an apartment, or even a room, in one of them, but they were always full up. Now they are gone, and a dull-faced educational edifice stands in their places. At that time and later, I tramped in and out of most of the handsome old houses on the north side of the Square, looking for a place to live. Some of those houses were demolished to make way for a set of brand-new, drearily uniform apartments, and most of the rest have been turned into offices. The hotel in which I now live is elderly, and last night I wondered, not for the first time, whether its last days might not be approaching. The pleasant side entrance has been sealed off, which is a discouraging sign.

I climbed in off the balcony and sat down on the comfortable little sofa that is the chief decoration of my sitting room. It is a nice room, with folding doors going into the bedroom. The fireplace no longer works, of course. I took the cards I had bought out of their box and looked at them. They were the shape and texture of playing cards, but instead of the hearts and diamonds and all, these cards were decorated with flowers and geometric designs. I wondered why I'd bought them. I was never enthusiastic about trying to build houses with cards.

I work in a building in midtown. My office is twenty stories up in the air, and from this eminence yesterday morning I watched the demolition of a red brick building far below. I must have stared down at the roof of that building a thousand times, but now that it was gone, I found I really could not recall what it looked like. In the afternoon, when I went to lunch, I found a whole block of

Sixth Avenue gone, and I hadn't any recollection at all of those vanished houses, except that I thought they might have been a reddish color. Or maybe they were gray. It is very disconcerting to have a gap suddenly appear in a spot where you can't remember ever having seen a wall.

The walls in my hotel rooms are a bright green-blue, a sort of bird's-egg color. It is a lovely color, although I would never have had the nerve to choose it myself if I had been painting the room. I always liked white walls, but I have grown very fond of this cheerful color. Now, looking at the walls, I found myself thinking they should be even brighter, with more blue in them, so that they'd really assert themselves. When? When the hotel comes down, as it seems bound to do. I saw the inside walls of the building that's coming down below my office today. Yellow, green, brown, ugly pale shades of those three colors, the walls made a poor show. They looked sad, as though they had never expected anything better than to be thrown away. This hotel room of mine won't look sad when they take the roof off. The tenants of the towering apartment building across the street are going to remark on this color. It will never be confused with the rubble that will litter the floor here.

I had white walls in the little Ninth Street apartment that was torn out from under me last year by the wreckers. My front windows peered up at a big, flat-fronted apartment building very similar to the one that faces me in the hotel here. I'm afraid my white walls must have looked forlorn when they were exposed to view. A blinding purple or a coat of scarlet might have saved them from nonentity.

I had been setting those grooved cards around on the table, looking at their patterns, but now I gathered them up and put them back in their box. It was too much. The city was tottering around me, the floor beneath my feet was already shivering under the wreckers' boots, so to speak, and I was about to build a house of cards that was guaranteed to stand. I was irritated by the picture, but it nagged at me. I wished I'd never seen the cards, with their bland, obvious little burden of intimations. Here I was admiring my room because it would look well after the roof was off. I was congratulating my room, and myself, because it would make a creditable corpse.

All my life, I suppose, I'll be scurrying out of buildings just ahead of the wreckers, and I can't afford to start wondering, every time I have the place painted, if the walls will speak up after the room has been laid open.

These cards might become a craze. I can see people all over the city sitting in doomed apartments building houses of cards that will last. And painting their walls in noisy colors to astonish the tenants of the high buildings around. Mass hysteria might set in, with the house painters celebrating. I'm going to give these cards away. I'll give them away separately and pretend they're bookmarks. I used to like to play patience, though. I might buy a set of plain old playing cards. No reflection, no significance, no fancies, just patience, and the game as I play it, impatiently, will be quite enough for me.

JULY 16, 1955

Lessons and Lessons and Then More Lessons

ON Eighth Street, in the Village, there is a modest restaurant, humanely lighted, not too bright and not too dark, where I used to spend about two hours every day, sometimes in the afternoon and sometimes in the evening, sitting always at a small table by the large street window. The window was recessed, and half curtained, and it was furnished with an oversized Tiffany lamp and an oversized bronze-colored crock that held artificial flowers or artificial leaves, according to the season of the year. I spent a good deal of time by that window. I remember being there on November nights when it was snowing, and all the people hurrying by were brightened by their white crowns and white epaulets, and then there were afternoons in midsummer when I hardly dared look out for fear of seeing some struggling man or woman become finally embedded in the thick heat, to vanish forever as I watched. I was such a faithful customer that a martini usually appeared on the table while I was still arranging my books in the order in which I would look at them.

There was a small service bar halfway down the room, which was very long and very narrow, but there was no place where people could just sit and drink. It was a decorous place, with exactly as much style as a nice, plain tearoom. I used to always carry three or four books with me, and if I had just visited the bookshop across the street, I often had six or more to look through when I was not attending to the outside scene.

One afternoon — it was autumn; there was an armful of flaming, papery leaves in the crock beside me — I glanced up to see two nuns walking by, walking west toward Sixth Avenue. All nuns look alike. Their black draperies, their resolute tread, and their remote air — everything about them was familiar to me. I was surprised to see them, as I am always surprised to see nuns abroad in New York, and I thought, as I had thought at other times, that it is out of the ordinary to see nuns here, and a very ordinary matter to see them in Dublin, where I was born. There was a time, during the years I spent in a convent boarding school and for many years afterward, when the sight of a nun would fill me with apprehensiveness and dislike, and I was glad then, sitting by that restaurant window, to know those years were gone.

That afternoon I had arrived at the restaurant when the lunch hour was over, and now, except for two waiters, the place was empty. I like empty restaurants, and I had counted on having all the tables and booths to myself. Even the cash register, by the door, was unguarded. I had taken the afternoon off, but why, what excuse I had offered myself, I can't remember. Perhaps I felt free because it was autumn again. Even so, three o'clock in the afternoon is no hour for anybody to be sitting at a window in a public restaurant with a martini in front of her, or half a martini, as it was by the time the nuns passed, and it seemed miraculous to be able to be so free and independent that I could be in the restaurant I preferred and drink what I liked and eat what I liked and read the books of my choice and see two nuns pass and feel nothing except a slight surprise — no apprehensiveness, no wild survey of a panicky conscience, nothing like that.

The two nuns who ran that boarding school were violent women. The head nun was short and fat and her assistant was tall and thin, and they both had genteel accents, the fat one speaking low, the thin one high. The head taught English and her assistant conducted singing classes, but they spent most of their time looking for sin. Their task was easy because of course we were all filled with sins, but they worked hard at it. They were always on patrol, sometimes together and sometimes separately. They patrolled the silent study hall, and they patrolled the corridors, and they patrolled the classrooms and the washrooms, and they even patrolled the dormitories, often walking between the beds after the lights were out. We knew what they were hunting for, of course, and as soon as one of them appeared in the doorway of a classroom, or anywhere, we all knew that sin had been stalked home and that at least one person in the room was going to have to

answer for herself. The only thing was, we did not know
which one of us it would be. I always felt I was the sinner,
and I suppose the others felt the same. The Devil works in
mysterious ways, and there was never any way of knowing
which of our faces he had chosen to reveal himself in. We
never knew where we were. Those two nuns tracked him
down even in the refractory, where we had breakfast, dinner, tea, and supper. They never seemed to notice what
was on our plates. Awful food. It was always tea and bread
scraped with butter, except at midday dinner, when it was
boiled potatoes. And at supper the tea was replaced with
vile cocoa. For breakfast on Mondays and Wednesdays
and Fridays, the tea and b & b were accompanied by one
tablespoonful of dates that had been boiled into a thin
soup, or, as the nun who cooked would have said, a jam.
On Tuesdays and Thursdays breakfast was emboldened by
a wafer of cold porridge damped with blue milk, on Saturdays by a spot of marmalade, and on Sundays by an ugly
morsel of bacon. Teatime and suppertime were all bread
and butter, except that at teatime we were allowed to bring
out the jam and cake we had received in packages from
home. Some girls got parcels from home and some didn't.
Those who did had the privilege of going around from
table to table (there were five long, narrow tables) carrying
pots of jam and big cakes and bestowing their favors on
the girls they liked and walking past the girls they didn't
like. There were about sixty of us, aged from seven to
eighteen, and sometimes the room was quite busy at teatime, especially at the beginning of each term, when eve-

rybody had something to walk about with. I can't remember Sunday dinner, but on Mondays and Wednesdays it was boiled potatoes with black pudding that was nearly all gray, and on Tuesdays and Thursdays it was said to be corned beef. On Fridays something fishy, and on Saturdays a stew — an end-of-the-week stew.

I was thinking of that Saturday stew and admiring the huge menu the waiter had left on my table when the entrance door of the restaurant opened and the two nuns walked in. They had been looking for a nice quiet place to eat, and they had found it. They walked quickly, without making a sound, straight down the restaurant, and I watched them all the way, and watched until they had settled themselves in a distant booth. Then I went back to my menu. The menu was still in my left hand, tilted up, as I had been holding it, but my right hand, with the empty martini glass in it, had somehow gone under the table and was hiding there behind the tablecloth. It was the moment of no comment. It was the moment of no comment.

NOVEMBER 10, 1962

A Snowy Night on West Forty-ninth Street

IT snowed all night last night, and the dawn, which came not as a brightening but as a gray and silent awakening, showed the city vague and passive as a conva-

lescent under light fields of snow that fell quickly and
steadily from an expressionless heaven. This Broadway
section where I live is all heights of roofs and all shapes of
walls all going in different directions and reaching different heights, and there are times when the whole area
seems to be a gigantic storehouse of stage flats and stage
props that are stacked together as economically as possible
and being put to use until something more substantial can
be built, something that will last. At night, when the
big Broadway lights go on, when the lights begin to run
around high in the sky and up and down the sides of
buildings, when rivers of lights start flowing along the
edges of roofs, and wreaths and diadems begin sparkling
from dark corners, and the windows of empty downtown
offices begin streaming with watery reflections of brilliance, at that time, when Broadway lights up to make a
nighttime empire out of the tumbledown, makeshift daytime world, a powdery pink glow rises up and spreads over
the whole area, a cloudy pink, an emanation, like a tent
made of air and color. Broadway lights and Broadway
nighttime color make a glittering spectacle that throws all
around it into darkness. The little side streets that live off
Broadway also live in the shadow of Broadway, and there
are times, looking from the windows of the hotel where I
live at present, on West Forty-ninth Street, when I think
that my hotel and all of us here on this street are behind
the world instead of in it. But tonight when I looked out
of these windows just before going to dinner I saw a

kaleidoscope out there, snow and lights whirling sky-high in a furious wind that seemed to have blown the Empire State Building clear out of the city, because it was not to be seen, although I had my usual good view of it this morning. It was a gray morning and the afternoon was gray, but tonight is very dark, and when I walked out of the hotel into the withering cold of this black-and-white night, West Forty-ninth Street seemed more than ever like an outpost, or a frontier street, or a one-street town that has been thrown together in excitement — a gold rush or an oil gush — and that will tumble into ruin when the excitement ends. This block, between Sixth and Seventh Avenues, exists only as a thoroughfare to Broadway, a small, narrow thoroughfare furnished with what was at hand — architectural remnants, architectural mistakes, and architectural experiments. The people who decided to put this street to use for the time that remains to it have behaved with the freedom of children playing in a junkyard. The houses and buildings are of all sizes, some thin and some fat, some ponderous and some small and humble, some that were built for grandeur at the turn of the century, like my hotel, which now has a neon sign hanging all down its fine, many-windowed front, and some that never could have been more than sheds, even if they are built out of cement. In the daytime and especially in the early morning the street has a travel-stained look and an air of hardship, and then the two rows of ill-matched, ill-assorted houses make me think of a team of worn-out horses, collected from everywhere, that are being worked for all the life that is left in them and that will have to keep going until their legs give out. Nobody will care when this street comes down because nobody really lives here. It is a street of restaurants, bars, cheap hotels, rooming houses, garages, all-night coffee shops, quick-lunch counters, delicatessens, short-lived travel agencies, and sightseeing buses, and there are a quick dry-cleaning place, a liquor store, a Chinese laundry, a record shop, a dubious movie house, a young, imperturbable gypsy who shifts her fortune-telling parlor from one doorway to another up and down the street, and a souvenir shop. The people who work here have their homes as far away from the street as they can possibly get, and the hotels and rooming houses are simply hotels and rooming houses, with tenants for a night or a week or a month or an hour, although there are a few old faithfuls who moved in for a little while and stayed on and on until the years turned them into permanent transients. The oldest houses on the street are four thin, retiring brownstones that still stand together on the north side, all of them with restaurants or bars on their ground floor. It was to one of these brownstone houses that I went for dinner tonight, to the Étoile de France. Above the restaurant all the floors of the house are abandoned, the windows staring blankly and the wall scarred, but the falling snow curtained the windows and shaped the roof so that the old house appeared once again as it did in its first snowstorm, when the street was new. I had walked along from the hotel, and I waited to cross over to the Étoile, but the cars were going wild, confined as they were to one uncertain lane by the mountains of snow piled up on both sides, and while I waited I looked back the length of the street. The bewildering snow gave the shabby street an air of melancholy that made it ageless, as it will someday appear in an old photograph. But it will have to be a very old photograph. The inquisitive and sympathetic eyes that will see this street again as I saw it tonight have not yet opened to look at anything in this world. It will have to be a very old photograph, deepened by time and by a regret that will have its source in the loss of all of New York as we know it now. Many trial cities, facsimiles of cities, will have been raised and torn down on Manhattan island before anybody begins to regret this version of West Forty-ninth Street, and perhaps the photograph will never be taken. But on the street level, Forty-ninth Street defied the snow, and business was garish as usual. The Étoile was very bright and cheerful when I walked in, but there were very few customers. There was only one man sitting, lounging sideways at the bar — an old Frenchman who comes in often at night, after having had his dinner at the Automat. Only three of the tables in the bar were occupied, and the big back room, the dining room, was dim and deserted. The Étoile is a very plain place, with plain wooden chairs, very hard chairs, red-and-white-checked tablecloths, a stamped tin ceiling painted cream, and wallpaper decorated with pale, romantic nineteenth-century

scenes. I sat at a table across from the bar, which has a long
mirror behind it to reflect the bottles and glasses and the
back of the bartender's head and the faces of the customers
and the romantic wallpaper on the wall behind me. One
waiter was still on duty — Robert — and he brought me a
martini and took my order and went off to the kitchen in a
hurry. I think the chef must have been making a fuss about
getting away early on this stormy night when there were
almost no customers and he was going to have trouble
getting home. He lives in Long Island City. Mme. Jacquin, who owns the restaurant, had gone home, and her
daughter, Mees Katie, was in charge, together with Leo,
the bartender. Leo has been working here about fifteen
years. He is Dutch, and I think he is in his late fifties,
a few years younger than Mme. Jacquin. Mees Katie is
about thirty. She has a singularly detached manner, as
though she were only working at the Étoile while she
waited for her chance to go to some place where she really
wants to be, but she spends more and more time here,
while her mother, who used to almost live in the place,
often does not come in for days at a time. Mees Katie
began coming in about five years ago to help during the
luncheon hour, but now she is here every night as well.
She leaves at ten o'clock, when the chef goes home, and
after that Leo manages by himself. On good nights the
bar is open until two in the morning, or even later.

Mees Katie was sitting as she always sits, facing toward
the door, so that she could jump up when the customers

came in. She often sits alone at the table for one by the street window, a huge window partly curtained in colorless gauze, and when there is a rush on, she stands in the arch that leads from the front room to the back and watches both rooms. She never sits at the bar. Tonight she was sitting beside a lady I have never seen at the Étoile before, a very wide, stout, elderly lady whose elaborate makeup — eyes, complexion, and mouth — looked as though it had been applied several days ago and then repaired here and there as patches of it wore off. Her hair was dyed gold and curled in tiny rings all over her head, and her face and neck were covered with a dark beige powder. Her face had spread so that it was very big, but her nose and mouth were quite small, and she had enormous brown eyes that had no light in them. She had put on a great deal of black mascara, and blue eyeshadow. The shadow had melted down into the corners of her eyes and settled into the wrinkles. She was all covered up in a closely fitted dark blue velvet dress that was cut into a ring around her neck and had long tight sleeves that strained at her arms every time she lifted her spoon to her mouth. She was eating pears in wine, and she ate very carefully, looking into the dish as she chose each morsel. When she wasn't attending to the pears, she watched the man sitting opposite Mees Katie, and she listened to him, and Mees Katie listened to him, and he listened to himself. His name is Michel, and he never stops talking. He has something to do with importing foreign movies, or with promoting them, and he is always busy. He is always on the run, going in all directions. He never finishes his dinner without jumping up from his chair at least once to dash into the back room, where the telephone is, to make a call, and it is always an urgent call. If the phone is busy, if there is someone ahead of him, he stands waiting impatiently in the arch between the two rooms, looking importantly about him, and when he has finally gotten into the telephone booth and put his call through, he keeps the door open until he is halfway through his conversation. His voice can be heard all over the restaurant until suddenly there is a little clatter as he shuts himself away with his secrets. He has a very high, harsh voice, and he twists each word so that only half of it sounds like English. Leo makes fun of him. Once, when Michel had pulled the phone booth door shut on himself, Leo called from the bar to Mees Katie, who was sitting at a table with some people, just as she was tonight, "Michel is talking with the weatherman again," and Mees Katie looked annoyed, although she smiled. She gets impatient with the Étoile, and with the people there, and especially with Michel, because he pesters her, but she has a kind heart, and she is always polite.

Michel always comes into the restaurant alone, looking for company, and once in a while when there is no acquaintance he can join for dinner he sits by himself. When he is alone, all his animation dies away and he looks old and tired. He has a very broad dark face, with loose wrinkles, furrows, running up and down it and overlapping its outline. His forehead is high, and he has kinky coal-black hair and a neat, thin mouth. When he sits at his table with nobody to talk to or to pay any attention to him, he looks deserted, as though he had been brought to the restaurant and left there by someone who had no intention of coming back to claim him. Alone, he is morose and dignified, as though humiliation had taken him unawares but had not found him unprepared. On nights like that, when he knows he is doomed to solitude, he stands at the bar with his drink, sweet vermouth, until his dinner is brought, and then he goes to his table and sits down very deliberately and shakes out his napkin very fussily. He places the napkin across his lap and folds it closely around him so that his jacket hangs free of it. He always wears a double-breasted suit, and a waistcoat. When the napkin is safely in place, he picks up his knife and fork and sounds all the food on his plate and looks severely at his green salad. Then he cuts off a piece of meat and places it in his mouth and begins to chew it. While he is chewing, his knife and fork lie on his plate, and his wrists rest against the edge of the table, with his hands limp, and he chews patiently, looking as proud and as indifferent as though he were facing a firing squad.

I think he must have had dinner alone tonight before I came in, and after dinner moved over to join Mees Katie and her acquaintance, the elderly painted lady. There was nothing, not even a glass of water, in front of Mees Katie and nothing in front of Michel, but the elderly lady's part of the tablecloth looked as though it had been thoroughly occupied by several different dishes before her pears in wine were brought. Mees Katie looked very tired. She has a lot of acquaintances, most of them inherited from her mother, and I suppose the elderly lady was one of them. Mees Katie has an attitude she falls into when she is being officially companionable. She sits with both elbows on the table, with her right hand placed flat against the side of her head and her left hand, with the fingers curled under, and turned down, supporting her chin. The right hand always holds her head up, while the left hand is ready to rise against her mouth, as though the polite attention she wants to give people calls for modesty from her, and for as complete a concealment of her own personality as she can manage. Tonight, as she listened wearily to Michel, her hand hid her mouth and her eyes were fixed on Michel's face. She is often bored, but as a rule she can escape from her entanglements by jumping up to greet a customer or to give an order to the waiter. There was no easy escape for her tonight — the Étoile might as well have been snowbound for all the coming and going there was. It was very quiet. Three men sitting at the last table in the bar were talking quietly, but the only voice really to be heard belonged to Michel, and Mees Katie kept her eyes fixed on him as though she feared she might fall asleep if she stopped watching him. She has extraordinary eyes, small slanted brown eyes that are filled with light, brilliant eyes of a transparent brown in which the color recedes, not growing darker but growing more intense, so that the point of truest color, the source of all that light, seems very far away, and perhaps it is for that reason that Mees Katie's expression always seems distant, no matter how close her face is as she bends down to answer a question or to whisper to some customer she knows well.

Suddenly the elderly lady finished her pears, and she laid down her spoon and smiled, a small, mild, accustomed smile of pleasure, and she turned to look at Mees Katie, and Mees Katie yawned and was shocked at herself.

"Oh, I am sorry, Michel!" she cried. "Excuse me, Mrs. Dolan, but I am so tired tonight."

Michel emerged from his monologue to see that he was in danger of losing his audience, and he looked over at Leo and called excitedly for cognac, cognac all round.

"Oh, no no no, thank you, Michel," Mees Katie said. "No cognac for me, thank you very much."

But Mrs. Dolan was delighted. She removed her lips from the edge of her coffee cup, which she was holding with both hands, and for a minute she looked like the perky little person she must once have been, who knew that at the mention of a drink a girl brightens up. "Well, thank you very much," she said to Michel, who had begun to stare at her with alarm. "I believe I will." She had a very loud, rusty voice, and after regarding Michel with approval she turned to Mees Katie. "Have a drink," she said. "A little cognac will settle your stomach."

Mees Katie laughed in a horrified way. "Oh, my stomach is all right," she cried, and she called to Leo, "M. Leo, *deux cognacs, si'l vous plait.*"

Mees Katie is tall and slender, and she moves very easily and quickly. She went to the bar and took the little tray with the two cognacs from Leo and handed it to Robert, who had come running from the end of the bar. Then she walked quickly away, through the bar and through the dim dining room, and pushed open one of the doors leading to the kitchen and went in there and stayed a few minutes. When she returned she was very brisk in her beaver hat and her beaver-lined coat. She said goodnight to Michel, who had become very glum, and to Mrs. Dolan, and to the old Frenchman at the bar, and to me, and she motioned Leo to the end of the bar and spoke a few words privately to him as she pulled on her gloves, and off she went. As she talked with Leo she stood sideways to the bar, and looked through the window, and a minute later, watching through the window, I saw her go past, walking carefully on the dangerous sidewalk, with her hand up to hold her hat against the wind. She and her mother have an apartment where they have lived for many years, far over on the west side, near Tenth Avenue. Leo also watched her through the window, and when she disappeared he stayed where he was and continued to watch. There is a big open garage across the street that has pushed itself through the buildings and now is open at each end, making an arcade and therefore a vista — you can see a little section of the Forty-eighth Street scene from this window here, and the

people walking along there, who almost never turn their
heads to look over in this direction, seem very far away,
and they seem to be walking faster and with more sense of
direction than the passersby immediately outside the window. Tonight was so blurred and wild you could see nothing much except movements of struggle out there, but Leo
continued to watch. The back of Leo's head is perfectly
flat, and his skin is putty-colored, but more white than
gray or beige. His features are thick and fleshy and very
clearly defined, the nose a wide triangle, the upper lip a
sharp bow. His eyes are small and blue, and his half smile,
for he never smiles right out, is always accompanied by
a deliberate glance in which suspicion and interest are
equally mixed. Sometimes the interest becomes dislike.
He is vain. He is slow-witted and not handsome, and he is
past sixty and a bit fat, and yet he wears the pleased,
secretive expression of a man who has always gotten along
very well with women. After a while he abandoned his
survey of the window and moved along to speak with the
old Frenchman. They spoke in French. The Frenchman
objects to hearing English spoken at the Étoile, and he
becomes very irritable when English-speaking strangers
try to strike up an acquaintance with him. The three men
at the end of the room left their table and moved across to
that end of the bar and called for drinks. They were irresolute. They were marooned in the city for the night, and
they had taken rooms at the Plymouth Hotel along the
street, and they wanted to be entertained without becom-

ing involved, and the evening was going flat on them. They had come to the Étoile for dinner because they often have lunch there and always imagined it to be a place where interesting people came at night — show people, artists and writers, people like that, or at least French people who would sit and stand around and talk excitedly as they did in the movies — but there was no one worth watching or listening to, and tomorrow night they drive home to Larchmont with a disappointed feeling that they will translate as knowledge — New York City is just as dull as anywhere else when you have nothing to do.

Michel was still talking, but warily. The last thing he wanted was to be left alone with a strange woman, and he felt it was no compliment to him to be seen drinking with a Mrs. Dolan. He hadn't touched his cognac. She took a businesslike sip from hers and set the glass back on the table. She had stopped listening to him, and now she was sizing him up. A smile kept coming and going on her face — it was her contribution to the conversation and her acknowledgment of it. But she was considering, or ruminating, and a little trick occurred to her. She smiled and put her finger against her lips as though Michel were a child who was talking too much. Michel stopped talking.

"Do you come here much?" Mrs. Dolan asked him. It wasn't much of a question but it was too personal for poor Michel. He began to answer her, and then instead he jumped up and clapped his hands to the sides of his head. It is the gesture he makes when he remembers an urgent phone call, or when he has to run out of the restaurant on an urgent errand. Mrs. Dolan stopped smiling, but she showed no surprise or embarrassment. She simply looked at him. He had to run out on an urgent errand, he said, but he would be back in ten minutes.

He always returns to the Étoile after these errands, but Mrs. Dolan didn't know that, and it was clear she didn't believe him. She went on looking at him. In his excitement he knocked his chair back, and it fell against the edge of my table. He turned ungracefully and caught the chair and straightened it, using both his hands. "Pardon, Madame," he said to me, gaily. He looked me in the eye and smiled at me. He was triumphant, or at least relieved, because he was managing to break away from Mrs. Dolan, and he was glad of the diversion, of the fallen chair, because it made his getaway easier, but he would have smiled anyway, challenging me or challenging anyone to ignore him. When he smiles, his dark, even teeth remain tightly closed because he must always remain on guard and must always show that he does not fear the snub he watches for. I said quickly, "It doesn't matter at all," and I was glad I did because, although he had already begun speaking to Mrs. Dolan again, he turned and nodded to me, and I knew I was forgiven for the sin I had not committed, of not recognizing him.

Then he bustled to the coatrack, beside where I was sitting, and began wrapping himself up in his warm clothes — his warm fur-collared overcoat and his fur hat

and his big gloves. Mrs. Dolan watched him as indiffer-
ently as though he were a stranger who had chanced to
share her table on a train journey, and, as she might in a
train, she turned her head from him to look at the view, in
this case the bar, Leo, the old Frenchman, and the three
exiles from Larchmont. Leo had a dour expression on his
face as he watched Michel, who looked happily back at
him and then looked at Mrs. Dolan and saw he had lost
her attention. He called to her, "You will wait? You will be
here? You will not run away?"

She looked at him stupidly, and I was surprised when
she answered him. "I'm not going anywhere," she said in
her dreadful voice.

Leo spoke up. "It is snowing out, Michel," he said.

Michel grinned at him. "Ten minutes!" he cried, and
vanished.

"That Michel is a great joker, he thinks," Leo said.

"You call him a joker?" Mrs. Dolan said loudly. "Some
joker, I'll say." But Leo ignored her, and she began rum-
maging in the huge leather handbag that was on the table
beside her, propped against the wall. She took out a mirror
and moved it about while she examined herself, her eyes,
her mouth, and her earrings, and then she took out a dark
red lipstick and smeared it thickly back and forth on her
mouth, and afterward, while she was putting the lipstick
away, she pressed her lips closely together. With her little
finger, she rubbed the lipstick smooth, and tidied the corners of her mouth, and when she had finished she cleaned

the color from her finger with her dinner napkin and took a tiny sip of her brandy, and glanced at Michel's brandy, which he had not touched. After that she sat gazing at the stained tablecloth, and from time to time she pursed her lips thoughtfully at something she saw there.

THERE are three young girls who have been coming to the Étoile for their Sunday dinner the last few months. They share an apartment on Forty-seventh, and they all work as secretaries. Lately one of them, Betty, has been dropping in alone, early in the evening, before ten o'clock. She never comes for dinner, and she never stays after Mees Katie has gone home. Betty is about five foot two, a brown-haired, blue-eyed, round-faced girl with a pretty figure and a pretty smile, who obviously enjoys being a friendly little child among the grownups. Her winter coat is dark green imitation fur, and she wears sweaters and skirts most of the time, schoolgirl clothes. She walks in timidly, as though she is not quite sure of her welcome, and then she sits up at the end of the bar and asks for a Perrier water and drinks it very slowly, making it last. She dreams of being an actress, but I think the part she dreams of playing is the part she plays as she sits up at the bar of the Étoile and sips her Perrier and stares wonderingly all about her. The Étoile reminds her of a waterfront café she saw once in a movie that starred Jean Gabin and that I think has now been remade to include a very

young unknown actress named Betty who sits at the bar
with a Perrier stealing the show, although she has nothing
to say and nothing to do except be herself, poor and alone
and very young. She always puts down a dollar to pay for
her Perrier, but Leo seldom takes the money, and if he
does take it he gives her another Perrier on the house.
Once or twice Betty has sat at Mees Katie's table and
helped her listen to Michel. She finds Michel very enter-
taining. Tonight she walked in shortly after Michel ran
out. She came in expectantly, almost laughing, walking out
of the snowstorm as though she were walking into a party.
She pulled off her scarf, shaking the snow from it, and as
she began to unbutton her coat she looked around for
Mees Katie. Leo had come to the end of the bar and was
watching her, smiling.

"Where is everybody?" she cried. "Where's Mees Katie?" She sat up at the bar and Leo poured a Perrier for her.

"I'm celebrating, Leo," she said. "This is my very first
snowstorm. The office let us off at three o'clock, and I
walked round and round and round, all by myself, celebrating all by myself, and then I went home and made
dinner, but I got so excited thinking about the snow I just
had to come out again and thought I'd come here and
see Mees Katie. I thought there'd be thousands of people
here. Oh, I wish it would snow for weeks and weeks. I just
can't bear for it to end. But after today I'm beginning to
think New Yorkers never really enjoy themselves. Nobody
seemed to be really enjoying the snow. I never saw such

people. All they could think about was getting home. Wouldn't you think a storm like this would wake everybody up? But all it does is put them to sleep. Such *people*."

"It does not put me to sleep, Betty," Leo said in his deliberate way.

"I wish it would snow for a year," Betty said.

"It will take something warmer than a snowstorm to put me to sleep, Betty," Leo said.

Betty laughed self-consciously and looked at Mrs. Dolan.

"Michel is a bad boy tonight, Betty," Leo said, and he also looked at Mrs. Dolan. "He told this lady he'd be back in ten minutes and it has been twenty."

"Nearly half an hour," Mrs. Dolan said disgustedly. "Nearly half an hour."

"He'll be back," Betty said. "Michel always comes back, doesn't he, Leo?"

"Oh, yes, Michel comes back," Leo said, and he put his hand on Betty's arm and leaned far across the bar and began whispering in her ear, or tried to begin whispering in her ear, because at the touch of his face against her hair she pulled roughly away and looked at him with such distaste that he stepped back. Then he went to the cash register and opened the drawer and began looking in at the money and pretending to count it. He was furious. If she had spent ten years pondering a way to express disgust, she could not have found a better way. Even if they had been alone, Leo would never have forgiven her, but the three lingering men were watching, and so was Mrs. Dolan.

Betty sat alone for a minute and then she took her Perrier and slipped down from her stool and walked over to Mrs. Dolan. Betty looked flustered, but she was smiling.

"May I sit down?" she asked Mrs. Dolan.

"Oh, please do," Mrs. Dolan said.

Betty sat down in Michel's chair, diagonally across from Mrs. Dolan. "Michel will be back soon," she said. "He always comes back."

"He left me sitting here like this," Mrs. Dolan said.

"Michel is really a sweet kind person when you get to know him," Betty said. "He's a darling, really."

Leo called out, "Miss Betty, you owe me sixty cents."

Betty looked over at him in surprise.

"You forgot to pay for your drink, little girl," he said, smiling, and he waved at Robert the waiter. Robert took Betty's dollar to the bar and brought her back her change. She had gotten very red.

"He needn't have shouted at me," she said to Mrs. Dolan. Mrs. Dolan said nothing.

Betty began talking. "This is the first big snow I've ever seen," she said. "I thought it would be like New Year's Eve here tonight, or something. When they first told us we were getting off early from the office I felt it was like a party or something, but then after I walked around a bit it seemed more like a disaster, and I kept wanting to get into the spirit of the thing. I felt very left out all day. I kept walking around."

When she fell silent, Mrs. Dolan still continued to watch her, but she said nothing. She had nothing to say, and nothing to give except her silence, and so she said nothing, and made no reply, and they sat without speaking until the silence they shared strengthened and expanded to enclose them both.

Not long ago I saw a photograph in the evening paper of a crowd of circus elephants gathered around a dying elephant, Flora, who had fallen and was lying on her side on the ground. The elephant closest to Flora was trying to revive her by blowing air into her open mouth with his trunk. The newspaper story said that all the elephants in the troupe took turns trying to save their dying comrade, and the story finished by saying, "This practice is instinctive among pachyderms."

But that practice, instinctive among pachyderms, that determination to win even a respite from death, is no more instinctive than the silence was that grew and turned into a lifeline between Betty and Mrs. Dolan, because their silence arose from a shame so deep that it was peace for them to sit in its silence, and to listen to this silence, which was only the silence of their own nature, of all they had in common. Mrs. Dolan's face grew ruminative, and Betty's profile suggested she was lost in recollections that were not unhappy.

Michel walked in, a snowman. He must have been

standing out in the open, or walking, ever since he left the restaurant. He stood still just inside the door and banged the palms of his gloves together and sent a fond glance at Mrs. Dolan and at Betty, who had turned to watch him. Michel was very pleased with the entrance he had made, and he looked as though he would like to go out and come back in again.

"Don Juan, he thinks he is," Mrs. Dolan growled.

Michel moved to the coatrack and began unwrapping himself. He was very slow about it, and all the time he was pulling off his gloves, and unwinding his scarf, and shaking his fur hat, he faced the room as though he faced a full-length mirror, and he smiled, watching all of us, but not as he would watch the mirror. At last he stood revealed in his navy-blue-and-brown-striped suit and his rings and his crinkly black hair and his bow tie, and he strolled back to his table and sat down beside Mrs. Dolan, and smiled sweetly at Betty, and picked up the cognac that had been waiting for him. When I left they were all ordering more drinks, and Mrs. Dolan had decided to switch to crème de menthe. The old Frenchman came out of his reverie and began looking unpleasantly at the three men who were chattering in English at the end of the bar, and I knew he was becoming happier. I paid my bill and left.

The self-service elevator at my hotel shivered piteously when I stepped into it, and hesitated before starting its painful ascent to the high floor where I live. That is as usual. The tiny, boxy elevator is as alien to this elegantly made hotel as the blue neon sign that winks on and off in front. A marble staircase winds all the way up through the heart of the building, and decorated windows over every stairwell still filter and color the light as they have done for more than sixty years. The fireplaces have all been blocked up long ago, but the rooms are very big and the ceilings are high and the walls shut out all sound. I looked again through the windows that give me my view of Broadway. Just below me, on Forty-eighth Street, on both sides of the street, a few small houses huddle together in the shadows, and from their low level other, newer walls rise higher and higher to the south and east, but tonight the big buildings, the giants that carry Manhattan's monumental broken skyline, were lost in fog. I could see only the little roofs below me and their neighbors immediately beyond, all of them under smooth snow that shaped them in the dark into separate triangles and squares and rectangles and slopes. The snow on Forty-eighth Street was rumpled, but there was no one in the street and the open parking lot was empty. To the right, Broadway was still lighted up as high as the sky, but the lights shone weakly, smothered in fog, except for the dazzling band of color that runs around the Latin Quarter, a few houses away from me. I pushed open the window. The cold air rushed in, but no noise. What sound there was was drugged, as though I was a hundred floors above the street instead of only eleven floors. The wind had died down, and the snow fell thickly, falling in large, calm flakes.

JANUARY 21, 1967

A Visitor from California

WE had a visitor from California on the Fifth
Avenue bus going downtown tonight — a very
young man who was seeing New York for the first time.
He joined a group of us who were waiting for the bus
outside the glass bank at Forty-third Street and Fifth
Avenue, and he arrived very suddenly, in haste, embracing
a flowing plastic bag that had clothes on wire hangers
inside it. He was also carrying a slim black case — a distinguished-looking case made of some rough leather —
and a bunch of flowers in a green paper cone. He wasn't
out of breath or flurried, and he didn't seem ill at ease, but
he looked quickly at each of us, as though he were wondering whether he had *gotten away with it*. It was exactly
as though he had been planning to hurry up like that and
stand with us, pretending he was one of us, or hoping he
was one of us. It was as though he had been hiding around
a corner, or in a parked car, or even under the street, in a
manhole, waiting for the one and only moment that would
be right for his arrival among us. There was nothing furtive about him, but he walked up in an unusual way, very
lightly and quickly, and then stood for a few seconds looking around at us all. There were about ten of us there
waiting for the bus, but for those few seconds we might
all have been standing in the middle of a desert, having
been brought together for a reason that was a secret to
us. When nothing happened, and nothing was said, the
young man began organizing himself — settling in. He

stepped to the nearest tree and hung his clothes on its
lowest branch, about five and a half feet from the ground.
It was gray and windy there on the corner of Forty-third
and Fifth. It was about seven o'clock — the tired end of a
long day — and nothing was happening at that busy intersection except that people were hurrying home. Sticking
out of the top of the young man's plastic bag as it hung on
the tree were two wire hangers. One had a short white
raincoat on it and the other a suit of light-colored clothes,
and the flimsy transparent envelope that enclosed them
was much too long, and fluttered piteously as it was blown
against the tree by the wind. With his clothes out of the
way, the young man was able to get his hands sorted out.
He was carrying the slim black case, which was just an
inch or so longer than an attaché case, in his left hand, and
at this point he transferred the flowers to his left hand as
well and stood very straight, waiting, as though the first
part of his plan had been carried out and the next part
might now begin. The flowers were deep in their cone of
green paper. I could not even see what kind of flowers they
were. The young man was tall and slender, with brown
hair and very pale, clear skin. He might have been nineteen, maybe twenty-one. He looked English, but I felt
perfectly sure that when he spoke he would speak in German — perhaps in Russian, but more likely in German.
He did not look as though English were his language. He
wore a navy blue suit with a snowy white shirt and had a
button-down collar, and his tie, which was navy blue, was

very long and hung straight down, without a pin or any-thing to hold it. His general appearance was astonishingly conventional, and his hair was so well cut and brushed that it looked old-fashioned on such a young man. *He* didn't look old-fashioned. He was a twentieth-century young man of no special vogue or group, and his bearing suggested that there had been a few exactly like him in every generation since the world began. He was a literary and historical figure of a young man, an eternal or ideal type, an apprentice hero, eligible in society, promising at the office, and doomed in wartime. His particular wars would have been the First World War and the Crusades. Among authors, Jane Austen knew him well, although he belongs more to Galsworthy than to her, and James Montgomery Flagg drew his likeness over and over and over again, most often in summertime settings: tennis, croquet, punting on the river, picnics on the lawn, bicycles with two sizes of wheels — one for show, one for balance. In the distant past he was much closer to Saint George than to Galahad, and he was definitely related to Rupert Brooke, Thomas Chatterton, and the innocent ones among the troubadours. I cannot remember him in Shakespeare, except perhaps as Rosalind, but Rosalind was arch and self-conscious, and this young man wore a very plain, solemn expression as he waited with the rest of us for the bus that would take us all downtown. The Fifth Avenue buses now turn off at different points on the way down the avenue, according to their different numbers, and it is all confusing where it used to be perfectly simple. Most of us were waiting for the No. 5. The No. 5 is the bus that in days past would have gone straight down the avenue and under the Washington Square Arch and into Washington Square Park and back uptown on Fifth Avenue again. You could stay on that bus all day, riding up and down Fifth Avenue. Now the downtown No. 5 bus turns east on Eighth Street and disappears, because Manhattan has been proclaimed a one-way city and we have to do as we are told and go in herds, all in the same direction. The only way to get uptown on Fifth Avenue these days is on foot. It is the same with most of the other avenues — most of them are one-way uptown or one-way downtown — and it is disconcerting, because half of the city is lost to all of us. It is as though we were allowed to see people only from the front or only from the back. It is also as though the city were standing still. The avenues are no longer great thoroughfares or boulevards to be gazed at and known but channels through which we are bundled as efficiently as possible. Well, the No. 5 finally came along and most of us climbed into it. The young man was the last to board, and he stood waiting his turn with his case and his bunch of flowers in his left hand and his clothes, in their fluttering envelope, held aloft in his right hand. He clambered up into the bus, looking all bones, as though he were climbing a stepladder that was not balanced against anything. He put his clothes on the seat next to the door and he spoke to the driver. "How much do I owe you?" he said. He spoke English naturally, and his voice, like his appearance, was unaccented except by its clarity. After paying his fare, he sat down in the second seat from the door, beside his clothes, which he propped up carefully to keep them from wrinkling. Then he set his case on the floor, behind his legs, and put the flowers down alongside the clothes. Before putting the flowers down, he turned the green paper cone up to his face and stared into it. When all his possessions were disposed of, he sat up straight and began staring across the bus and through the opposite window, and he turned his head and looked through the front window, which gave him the driver's long view of the avenue ahead.

Our bus was going as fast as it could down the middle of the island, and all that the young man could see were closed buildings and hurrying forms on the sidewalks, and he was afraid he was missing something. And he was anxious. He turned to a lady next to him and said that he wanted to go to Ninth Street. He said, "I told the driver to let me off there. I hope he doesn't forget." Before we reached Lord & Taylor, the lady and all the rest of us who were close by knew that the young man was from California and that it was his first visit to New York. "It is very nice here," the lady said. "It is a nice place." She asked him no questions. She seemed not to want to talk to him, and her manner toward him was more one of patience than anything else. She was very tired. She was about sixty-five, and she wore her clothes as though she did not care what she wore or how she looked. There was a turban of dark gold bound around her gray hair, and she wore a brown suit, and black shoes and gloves. She had a huge, bulging handbag of black alligator, and she also carried a manila envelope that was too full of papers to be fastened, and two books — one a study of marriage and divorce in the United States and the other a paperback detective story by John Dickson Carr. She had no interest in the young man or in anyone else. He spoke rapidly, in a pleasant voice, telling her that he was going to 21 East Ninth Street and that New York was strange after the other cities he had seen. The bus became crowded, and although several people glanced at the seat that was occupied by his clothes, he made no gesture toward gathering the clothes and the flowers into his lap and did not seem to notice that there were almost no seats left vacant. He was unquestionably well brought up, and he must have been exceedingly valuable to the people who brought him up. He thought highly of himself, and although he was unassuming, he was not modest. Someone must have told him that all he had to do was be himself and things would go all right, and he was being himself — unassuming but not modest. He was very handsome except for his nose, which, like Marilyn Monroe's nose, was indefinite, and blurred almost to thickness. But Marilyn Monroe's nose made her beauty even more touching than it might have been if her face had been perfect, and the young man's nose saved his face from prettiness. His eyes were brown and wide open, and blankly attentive, like the eyes of some children when they are alone among the grownups and listening hard at some solemn occasion — a funeral or a wedding. When we came to Twenty-third Street, he said to the tired lady, "What's that?"

"What's what?" she asked.

"I thought I saw a park," he said.

"Oh, the park," she said, but she could not remember the name of Madison Square Park, and, in her annoyance, she roused herself enough to look out and say, "That's the Flatiron Building."

"The what building?" he asked.

"The Flatiron Building, because it's shaped like a flatiron."

"Like a flat what?" he asked.

"A flat *iron*," she said. Then she said "Flat i-r-o-n. Flat-iron, like a flatiron."

"Oh, yes," he said, and he stretched his neck to look at the red glass panel in the window of the cigar store on the ground floor of the Flatiron Building, which we were just passing. "It's very odd," he said politely.

The tired lady did not tell him that at Twenty-third Street we began riding through one of Fifth Avenue's most dismal stretches — a perfectly plain and forthright commercial area, with nearly all the buildings dating from the last century, which becomes so bleak and lonely when working hours are over that it is hard to walk through there on a holiday or a Sunday. But Fourteenth Street is all shops and bright lights, and seems like the beginning of a friendlier country. The young man saw the change and started looking over his shoulder to see if he could read the street names. "I don't want to miss my stop," he said. And the tired lady broke down and gave him the information she had been trying to keep to herself. "I get off at your stop," she said. When he heard that, he settled back, but he kept his head turned to watch the avenue approaching and vanishing as we rode along. He saw the Washington Square Arch ahead and remarked on it, and was not told that it does not make as fine a sight as it used to, since the high new buildings have risen up behind it south of the square. The bus pulled up at the Fifth Avenue Hotel, and the young man was the last to get off. He climbed down as he had climbed up, with his clothes aloft in his right hand and the flowers and the case clutched in his left hand. He stepped onto the sidewalk distrustfully, as though he feared it might be moving, and he looked down at his feet and at his flowers. "I hope I haven't forgotten anything," he said. The tired lady was walking away from him, but she turned back when she heard his voice. "Have you got your flowers?" she asked. She showed him the corner to wait on until the light changed and said firmly, "It will take you exactly two minutes to reach No. 21." And without a goodbye she vanished, hurrying away on West Ninth Street into the shadows along the wall of the Fifth Avenue Hotel. The last I saw of the young man, he was crossing Fifth Avenue under full sail, walking as lightly and as quickly as when he had joined the crowd of us outside the glass bank. There was nothing out of the way about him. He was a Californian visiting New York for the first time, and what was foreign about him was that he was just what he seemed to be — not merely a stranger but the Perfect Stranger.

JULY 19, 1969

Just a Pair of Show-Offs

I AM sure you have heard about those "flirty, flirty guys with their flirty, flirty eyes." They are in a song called "Paper Doll." I had an encounter with two of those flirty guys on Sixth Avenue tonight, and I am going to tell you about it. It was around nine o'clock when I met them. The rain that had fallen all day today had stopped, leaving the air damp and the streets wet and shiny, tinted with city lights. I was walking home after having dinner at the Lobster, on West Forty-fifth Street. I must say that that block of Forty-fifth, between Sixth Avenue and Broadway, is in terrible shape. It is something over two years since the wreckers moved in on the neighboring streets to the north, and now that the demolition is complete from Fiftieth Street all the way down to Forty-sixth, and the new skyscrapers are beginning to shoot up there, the few side streets that were spared, including Forty-fifth Street, look

outcast. The familiar theaters and restaurants are still going strong, but the streets they stand on have taken on the
appearance of slums. There have been a lot of changes. As
the streets became ravaged, an army of new girls, of all
shades and colors, arrived to walk around on them, and for
over a year now Sixth Avenue has been monopolized by
young — very young — black girls in huge gold and silver
wigs who are so theatrical and new-looking that when
you see them posing around the edge of the smelly ruins
and excavations you begin to wonder if the entire city is
rehearsing for some mad extravaganza that will end by
launching us all into Bedlam. I have to remark that Bedlam is the word you see around this midtown area these
days. You see it over and over again, inside and outside
the construction sites. You see it stamped in big letters on
motors and on the steel frames that will support those
skyscraper tons of concrete and glass and so on — Bethlehem, Bethlehem, Bethlehem. Whatever happens, we
won't be able to say we weren't warned by the manufac-
turer. When I reached the corner of Sixth Avenue and
Forty-fifth tonight, I saw that five or six of these brightly
wigged young girls had gathered in front of the greeting-
card shop, which was closed but which remains well
lighted after closing time. With the exception of the delicatessen, the other shops in the block were also closed, and
in some cases barred. There are a record shop, a shop that
sells old movie stills and photographs of movie stars (especially of dead movie stars), a cut-rate drugstore, a coin

shop, and a dress shop, but they were all dark. The greeting-card shop has two show windows flanking a recessed
glass entrance door. Two of the girls stood side by side in
this recess, making a centerpiece for their companions,
who had composed themselves into a group nice enough
to be the finale of *No, No, Nanette,* although their dress
seemed to promise a particularly subtle interpretation of
Gaîté Parisienne. Legs, coats, and heads they were, their
legs bare to the top, their coats tiny and black, and their
heads very big and high in their gold and silver wigs. They
all wore low-heeled shoes in light colors — gold and silver, mostly. I walked past them and on to the corner, where
the two flirts showed up — loomed up before me as I
stood at the curb waiting for the light to change. They
were about nineteen years of age, stocky fellows, and they
wore their raincoats buttoned up to the neck. They looked
alike, with round faces and peachy complexions and crew-
cut blond heads, and they were both grinning. They spoke
to me, making a suggestion to which I had no reply, although they must have hoped for one, because they waited
beside me until the light changed and I fled across the
avenue. After I had walked a few steps, I looked back to
see if anything was happening over there where the girls
were. Something was happening, all right. In the short
time since I left them, the two raincoats had not merely
reached the greeting-card shop but usurped the girls' place
in the doorway, and now they stood side by side in the
lighted recess, still grinning while they watched the girls,

who had moved off and were conferring together before scattering up and down the street. I was a bit puzzled. Those girls are not meek, yet they had seemed to give in very easily. Probably they have been instructed to avoid trouble, and they could hardly expect to do much business with those two idiots grinning in the background. I suppose there is a chance that the two flirts were in charge of the girls, but somehow I think that they were just a pair of show-offs, and that they drove the girls away. The last I saw of them all, the boys were still standing in the doorway, their round blond heads turning right, left, right, left as they enjoyed the view, and the girls were in full flight, hurrying along the wet pavement to their new stations.

NOVEMBER 15, 1969

On the Island

TONIGHT I stood on the traffic island in the middle of Broadway at Forty-fifth Street and watched a respectably dressed middle-aged woman sing "Bei Mir Bist Du Schön" at the top of her lungs to an audience she alone could see. She was blind drunk, and from the sullen expression on her face I would say she wasn't enjoying herself much. Her face was dark red, and on her short gray-black hair she wore a tiny hat of navy blue felt trimmed with stiff net. She hadn't enough breath to belt out the song, as she was trying to do, so she screamed the words in a hoarse voice that was colored more by bitterness and defiance than by music, but she kept good time with her umbrella, which she held high, pointed at the hoarding over the marquee of the Astor Theatre. Her hand seemed a lot steadier on the umbrella than her feet were on the ground, and as she sang and waved she did little bumps and grinds with a desperate coquetry that shamed her matronly dress and the sensible black shoes she wore. The last word of each line was a high point:

> *Bei mir bist du schön*
> Means that you're *grand,*
> *Bei mir bist du schön* . . .
> It means you're the fairest in the *land.*

There were thousands of people on the street. It was just past seven o'clock, and Broadway was well into the evening phase of her everlasting rush hour. The sidewalks were so jammed that you wouldn't think there was room for one more pair of feet, and on each side of the traffic island the cars raced by, going downtown, speeding for the Battery with the green light all the way, it seemed. But the traffic island was very solid, and even seemed quiet and in darkness, as though the roar and the blazing lights and the frantic movement all around had swallowed it up and made it invisible. There were three of us waiting there besides the drunken woman, but we stood on the safe part, where the cement base of the island widens out to form a little platform, and she was balanced on the narrow runway outside the low cement wall of the "flower bed," where bits of shrubbery wither in a small wasteland of tin cans and wine bottles and dirty scraps of cloth and paper. It seemed she must either fall forward under the wheels of the cars or fall backward into the rubbish, but she kept her feet somehow. Her umbrella (of beige silk, to match her gloves) was very long and thin and excessively pointed, and her manner with it was vigorous. There was a lot of punch in the way she waved it. The three of us standing on the island with her were just as much afraid of her as we were afraid for her. We just stood and watched her and wished the light would change, so that we might all be released from our oasis. I had seen her a few minutes earlier, on the east side of Broadway, near Forty-eighth Street. We walked alongside each other there for a minute, pressed together by the great crowd. It was a night to be outside. There was that curious feeling along Broadway of walking through darkness while being transfixed by lights that are too bright and not friendly. Those powerful store-front lights and cinema lights are meant for merchandise, not for human beings, and as we pushed along there the deep-dyed neon rays of red and green and blue and white gave each face in the crowd a family likeness, so we all seemed to be related — dubious, discolored copies of one another. I first noticed the woman next to me because of the exhausted way she put her feet to the ground, and when I looked at her face I saw that she was drunk, but although she didn't seem conscious of the people around

her she didn't seem lost. She seemed to know where she
was, all right, as though she took the same route every
night on her way home from work. She had a dull, sad
face, the face of a derelict who is able to recognize only
what is hateful to her, and which would change in sobriety
only to grow watchful and, so, harder. She looked about
fifty-five. Her figure was heavy in her navy blue winter
coat, and she carried a huge black leather handbag with a
copy of the *Post* fitted into its side pocket. As soon as I saw
an opening in the wall of backs ahead of me, I hurried
forward, and I didn't see the woman again until she appeared on the edge of the traffic island and began to sing.
When the light changed at last, the car that drew up
alongside her was a taxi, and as soon as it stopped she
slammed her umbrella down flat on the top of it and
began staring in at the driver. He prudently raised his arm
and grabbed the umbrella and held it tight against the top
of the cab, so that she couldn't lift it or pull it free. "Come
on, lady," he said. He was grinning, but he looked worried.
I crossed over to the sidewalk and went along to the
bookshop next door to the waxworks museum. It is really
not a bookshop but a high-ceilinged cavern stocked with
posters and pennants and buttons and all the queer objects
manufacturers devise for sale as souvenirs. At the back
there is a small book section, with cheap sets of the clas-
sics, and popular works on psychology, and paperbacks. I
looked until I found a Dorothy Sayers. I took my time,
because I didn't want to go outside and see that woman
again. When I finally went out, there was no sign of her.

She was gone, or if she was nearby she was quiet. At any rate, she was no longer in her place on the traffic island. I wonder about her, and how she came to be helpless like that in public. I wonder at the power of her nightmare — that it could wait for years and then trap her when she was finding her way home. I wonder how much of all this she will remember tomorrow. Not much, I think. Kind memory will fail her to save her for another day. She will say, "Oh, what a blackout I had last night!" I think that by tomorrow she will have quite forgotten the dangers she survived and the adventures she made for herself on her way home tonight.

JANUARY 10, 1970

Cold Morning

IT is ten degrees above zero, five o'clock in the morning, and I have just returned to this hotel after a visit to Bickford's, where I had a cup of coffee. I had to get the elevator man to let me out of the hotel. The outer doors are locked for security reasons, and in the little vestibule between the inner and outer doors such a blast of hot air was pouring up that I was glad to get out of it into the icy cold outside. There is no wind. The morning is still and dark, with the touch of anxiety that comes with waiting. It is time for the day to begin. For the moment, as I hurried around the corner to reach brightly lighted Bickford's as quickly as possible, I saw that the avenue — Sixth Avenue — was swept clean of traffic and pedestrians. It was a tall angular oasis of stillness, very hard and remote in outline but not unfriendly. I couldn't even hear my own footsteps. I am wearing fur mukluks I bought at Lord & Taylor, and I pad along making no sound. I didn't look up at the sky to see if I could find moon or stars, but I did take a quick look back up along Sixth Avenue and saw that uptown a little forest of Christmas trees was still glimmering whitely, seeming tall even against the high glass cliffs that ought to dwarf it.

Bickford's, which used to be a place of gay pastel plastic décor and bucket-shaped seats, is now comparatively somber, with shiny brown paneling on the walls, and countrified wooden stools, but the background array of jello and pie and fruit salad is as dominant as always, and the orange juice still bubbles away in its big glass dome. And the coffee is very hot. The waitresses wear white nylon uniforms, with woolly colored cardigans to ward off the drafts. My waitress was a middle-aged woman with gray hair and a hard, kind face. She told me she was very tired. "I'm not used to night work," she said. She brought over one of those heavy metal baskets of glasses to be put away, and as she set it down she knocked her elbow against the edge of the basket, hurting herself. "See, knocked my funnybone," she said as she rubbed her elbow. "I'm asleep on my feet. I'm not used to night work. That's what I'm telling you. I've been working days always." Bickford's was well lighted, as usual, but it was quiet there. About fifteen

customers stood or sat around, scattered here and there at
the counters, some of them talking in murmurs and some
of them stony still, with their hands holding their coffee
cups. One man was fast asleep with his face in the *Daily
News.* A thin woman in a drab brown coat and with a little
brown hat on her head was making a telephone call. It was
so dark and cold outside, and so quiet, so warm and quiet,
inside, that we all seemed to be sitting in the half-light —
a sequestered feeling.

When I finished my coffee, I thought of having a second cup, but I didn't. Bickford's seemed sad, in contrast to
its usual brassy air, and I didn't want to stay there. I hurried
along Sixth Avenue, and there were two people ahead of
me — a man and a woman with their arms around each
other's shoulders but walking quite quickly just the same.
They were in haste, and I got the impression they had a
long way to go. I rang the bell to get back into the hotel,
and this time I was glad of that blast of warm air in the
little vestibule.

JANUARY 20, 1973

A Daydream

THIS is a daydream: I am lying in the sand just below
the dunes on the beach in East Hampton, where I
lived for several years. It is a warm, sunless day, with a cool
breeze blowing in from the ocean. My eyes are closed. I

like the beach, and the sand. There is a big Turkish towel between me and the sand, and I am quite alone. The cats and my dog, Bluebell, walked over here with me, but two of the cats dropped out at the walled rose garden a short distance back, and the four others are hiding in the long dune grass just above me. Bluebell is down by the water. She is a black Labrador retriever, and she swims and rolls in the water and watches for a seagull to play with, but the gulls fly off shrieking with outrage at the sight of her. I won't stay here much longer. In a few minutes, I'll get up and start for home — a five-minute walk through dune grass and between trees and across the wide, sloping lawn that leads to the big house where the walled rose garden is. I live at the foot of that lawn. I'll just lie here a few more minutes and then I'll go back.

But I opened my eyes too suddenly, for no reason at all, and the beach at East Hampton has vanished, along with Bluebell and the cats, all of them dead for years now. The Turkish towel is in reality the nubbly white counterpane of the bed I am lying on, and the cool ocean breeze is being provided by the blessed air conditioner. It is ninety-three degrees outside — a terrible day in New York City. So much for my daydream of sand and sea and roses. The daydream was, after all, only a mild attack of homesickness. The reason it was a mild attack instead of a fierce one is that there are a number of places I am homesick for. East Hampton is only one of them.

SEPTEMBER 20, 1976

A Blessing

I THOUGHT if I got the three words "cold and sunny" into a first sentence, I could write you a letter. And there you are. I did it. I have no news, only a few observations and they are not even random observations. They are very solid observations, and if I am not careful they will hem me in and eventually turn into secrets and then, worse and worse, into convictions.

Thirty minutes later. I went off to make some coffee for myself, and while I waited for the water to boil I considered all the nonrandom "observations" I had so portentously lined up for your inspection. While I looked them over, they began to vanish, and finally they had all vanished — all gone, and a good thing, too. They would have made very dull reading.

They were a stilted crowd and rather disagreeable, as though they had found themselves at a party that was not quite what they'd expected and where their clothes were all wrong. They all wore elaborate taffeta ball gowns that seemed to belong to the eighteenth century, and each ball gown was a different shade of green.

They vanished one by one, but their departure seemed sudden, and I think now that they weren't observations at all but complaints, and, if so, they have gone into the complaints department, where I never look around at all. I am never to be found anywhere near the complaints department. There are too many mirrors in there for my liking.

The complaints department becomes empty every once in a while — stone-cold empty, and quite deserted. I always know when it is empty. When I am happy, I know that it is empty. That is, when I am especially happy. Furthermore, I believe that all the unhappy ones in there in that dismal department then turn into angels, or into something like angels, and go far, far away.

Yesterday afternoon, as I walked along Forty-second Street directly across from Bryant Park, I saw a three-cornered shadow on the pavement in the angle where two walls meet. I didn't step on the shadow, but I stood a minute in the thin winter sunlight and looked at it. I recognized it at once. It was exactly the same shadow that used to fall on the cement part of our garden in Dublin, more than fifty-five years ago.

We lived in that house thirteen years. It was one of a long row of houses that faced, across the quiet little street, another long row of houses, just like them, each with a little front garden and a good-sized back garden. Every time my father came into the house, coming home, he went first into the back sitting room to look through the big window at his wife's garden and see for himself what changes she had made there during the hours he had been away.

I celebrated my fifth birthday in that house, and I also celebrated my seventeenth birthday there, and I feel absolutely impelled to tell you that five is closer to seventeen than seventeen is to five. What do you think of that? And, of course, all my birthdays between five and seventeen were celebrated there. The birthdays of all of us were celebrated with presents in the morning and a very special birthday-cake high tea in the evening.

One New Year's Eve, something marvelous happened on our little street. It wasn't called a street; it was called an avenue. Cherryfield Avenue. And it was closed at the far end — no "thru" traffic. What happened that New Year's Eve was that in the late afternoon word went around from house to house that a minute or so before midnight we would all step out into our front gardens, or even into the street, leaving the front doors open, so that the light streamed out after us, and there we would wait to hear the bells ringing in the New Year. I nearly went mad with excitement and happiness. I know I jumped for joy. That New Year's Eve was one of the great occasions of our lives.

I must tell you now that I am praying to Almighty God for blessings on your house, with extra blessings to go with you whenever you leave the house, so that wherever you are you will be safe.

Blessings on your house. Happy New Year.

JANUARY 5, 1981